DOING BUSINESS IN THE BLACK COMMUNITY

GETTING IT RIGHT

Praise for Doing Business in the Black Community

"Doing Business in the Black Community skillfully guides readers through the intricate landscape of black businesses' challenges worldwide. Your ability to outline these issues while maintaining reader engagement is remarkable.

The incorporation of personal anecdotes and respondent scenarios adds a human touch, vividly illustrating the struggles and triumphs. This technique not only educates but also deeply resonates. Your book is a valuable resource, thoughtfully composed to inform and inspire, that will truly connect with its audience".

- Jessie Raymond, book editor.

DOING BUSINESS IN THE BLACK COMMUNITY

GETTING IT RIGHT

F B LAWRENCE

This business non-fiction book is based on actual events. All names, characters, places, and incidents have been altered for artistic and thematic purposes.

ISBN: 978-1-739-4350-8-0

Disclaimer

It is hereby acknowledged that the information used in the book has come from a variety of sources. No attempt has been made to misuse information but only to enlighten the audience. Every attempt has also been made to avoid the
infringement of any copyright.
Any perceived infringement is therefore unintended and regretted. The use of any of the contents of the book other than for educational purposes requires express permission of the publishers.

Published in the United Kingdom in 2023 by Framichi publications.

www.framichipublications.com

DEDICATION

The book is dedicated to all the amazing black entrepreneurs who are conducting their businesses in a professional and exemplary manner to make our black community proud.

I also dedicate this book to those black customers with the 'Black-First' mindset because they put black businesses first and consistently patronise them no matter what.

These two groups contribute to the economic empowerment of our black community.

FOREWORD

Written by Victor Ben Okoh

- *CEO/FOUNDER, VBO EXCLUSIVE LOUNGE*

- (London, United Kingdom).

Not much has been written about doing business in our black community. That is why this book is much needed and timely.

F B Lawrence's book brilliantly covers the valuable feedback from black customers on one hand and the challenges faced by black entrepreneurs on the other because both sides need to be heard.

Entrepreneurs are striving to run a successful business and they require support from our community. It is important that we are able to understand, encourage, and support each other. Black entrepreneurs to other entrepreneurs. Customers to entrepreneurs and entrepreneurs to customers.

Since entrepreneurs are also customers, it is important that they are receptive to any customer feedback received. Do not disregard customers' feedback in this book. Tick the box and if there is anything to be fixed, use it to improve your business. You will be glad you did because this book is full of fantastic nuggets on HOW TO GET IT RIGHT.

My advice to black entrepreneurs is to conduct market research and a feasibility study before jumping into any new business. Do not copy another business unless you have the full picture. Entrepreneurs should also adhere to the legislative requirements relevant to their business sector to ensure they are eligible for business finance and other available support.

Lastly, reinvest in your business because it is important to continuously upgrade and refresh your business. This is crucial for success.

I recommend this book to everyone in our black community, especially upcoming entrepreneurs, and business owners as it would improve the way we conduct business now and in the future.

ACKNOWLEDGEMENT

This book was made possible by the incredibly knowledgeable people I had the opportunity and privilege to interview in my research. I put out a request for interviewees and these lovely people responded from all over the world; Europe, USA, Canada, the Caribbean and Africa. This book is full of your stories and experiences and I hope I did them justice.

- Augusta Osayande
- Austin Gbuji
- Bolaji Eyo
- Carmen Cameron
- Conrad Ononeme
- Dr Dorothy Okwuchi
- Dr Ifeoma Ogosi
- Dr Michael Ikumobasin

- Dr Presley Omoruyi
- Dotun Zubair
- Della Wesa
- Ed Enabulele
- Efe Durosinmi-Etti
- Enoor Osubele
- Lance Kadiri
- Mark De Couteau
- Mike Kasibo
- Mariam Sholaja
- Nana E Fynn
- Nana Owusu-Adjei
- Patrice Bailey
- Patricia Osazuwa
- Patrick Spencer Salami
- Reggie Arutoghor
- Richard George
- Sammie Omotese
- Shola Sodiya
- Stella Osakwe
- Sunny Ologun

- Tina Ogunremi
- Victor Ben Okoh

I must also thank some of my friends, Ed, Shola, Anthony, Remi, Efe and Lance. They were a brilliant sounding board for the various ideas and topics in this book. They got on a call with me anytime I needed to discuss all aspects of the book writing, publishing, and book launch process.

A big thank you to Mr Victor Ben Okoh for taking time out of his very busy schedule to write such a befitting Foreword for this book. I appreciate it.

This book looks as good as it does because of the expertise of the Framichi Publications freelance production team. Thank you, Rose, Isa and Jessie for the beautiful book cover, proofreading, formatting, and interior layout design. You are the best and such a pleasure to work it.

TABLE OF CONTENTS

WHY THIS BOOK?

My answer is why not? I think it is about time a book was written about the peculiarities of doing business in our black community. We are inundated with social media posts every day, asking us to support black businesses. I have had numerous debates with friends, colleagues and relatives about the issues preventing some people in our community from patronising black businesses. Many of my friends and I have experienced these issues first-hand and discussed them at length.

I also belong to a few black professional communities where this has become a recurrent topic. These are the usual questions raised:

- Why do black businesses expect black people to patronise them just because we are all black people or belong to the same ethnic group?
- Why do they have this sense of entitlement that we must be our 'brothers' keepers?'
- Of course, we want to support black businesses, but what happens if the services and products are below standard and put customers off?

Like me, many believed that black businesses have to provide good services and products to attract and retain customers. That is the first step. The experience of many of us in the black community is often quite disappointing and negative. I am not saying only black businesses offer poor services and products because it happens to businesses in other ethnic communities too.

The difference is what happens after a customer has received poor service. There should be damage control as soon as possible. In my experience, which has been corroborated by the outcome of my research, not much effort is made by most black businesses to 'fix it', and they end up losing the customer or any repeat business. In addition, an angry customer spreads the bad feedback far and wide and that affects the business in question.

So, who is listening? Are the businesses listening to us? Are they making the necessary changes to ensure CUSTOMER SATISFACTION AND REPEAT BUSINESS?

After another unpleasant experience a group of us had with a black business, a friend asked me to write this book. My reluctance to write this book disappeared after one year of conducting thorough research and analysis of the way we do business in our community.

I interviewed black people worldwide and they were very keen to share their experiences and stories of dealing with black businesses. I put out an ad on my social media pages for anyone willing to share their experiences and perspectives on black businesses to contact me, and I received many responses from people in our community who wanted to have their say on this topic. I circulated a questionnaire and received the same enthusiasm from respondents; everyone offered their opinion freely. I concluded that we had serious problems that needed to be addressed and difficult conversations to have as a community. What better way to kickstart this movement than to write a book that can reach the black community worldwide?

In this book, I have explored the prevalent issues with various black businesses in our community, as recounted by various customers. I will also make recommendations on how to get it right to ensure consistency and repeat business.

My research was not one-sided. I wanted a balanced approach, so I also interviewed black businesses to understand their pain points and challenges with doing business in the community. What do they think of black customers? The feedback was enlightening. I think there is a lot we can do to make it easier for businesses to serve us too.

According to my father, "Only a fool generalises." Therefore, it would be foolish to paint all black businesses with the same negative brush. To that end, I must point out that **this is a general impression about black businesses, but it does not mean there are no excellent black businesses out there with professional conduct.** There are also many award-winning black businesses. There are just not many of them and we wish there were.

The negative feedback is quite troubling and completely overshadows the positive, and that is what we need to fix. I bet you will read this book and nod in agreement on most, if not all its pages because it says it exactly as it is. All the respondents from all over the world said pretty much the same thing. Can they all be wrong?

It is time for businesses to do an introspection and reflect on why their businesses fail to attract enough customers and eventually become unsuccessful.

My research revealed a few schools of thought, which I have separated into different categories for the purpose of clarity.

- Black businesses only care about making money as quickly as possible.
- Black people cannot collaborate because we are programmed to compete.
- A lack of education/business acumen is to blame.
- We are overly critical of black businesses.
- Black businesses do not fully understand customer service.
- Black businesses have a nonchalant attitude to professionalism.
- There's distrust and negative preconceptions of black businesses.
- Black businesses are too lazy to make money.

- Black businesses take black customers for granted.
- Black customers take black businesses for granted.
- Black businesses cannot obtain finance from banks due to prejudice.
- Black people cannot do business.

Are these schools of thought, correct? Do you agree with any of them? Well, keep reading and you can make up your mind about that.

The issues with doing business in our community has often been described as a mindset problem that would take a paradigm shift to change. How do we change the mindset of an ethnic group that is spread all over the world? Who knows, maybe this book would help to steer us on the right path.

Since entrepreneurs are also customers, I am hopeful that black business owners will read this book and decide that it is time to reflect on this feedback from black customers and do an introspection to determine how they can improve on all the issues raised by customers. On the other side of the spectrum, I hope black customers will empathise with black businesses and give them more opportunities to get it right.

That is my objective for writing this book which I call a FREE market research, and my 'gift' to my community.

PART ONE

Black Customers Share Their Pain Points

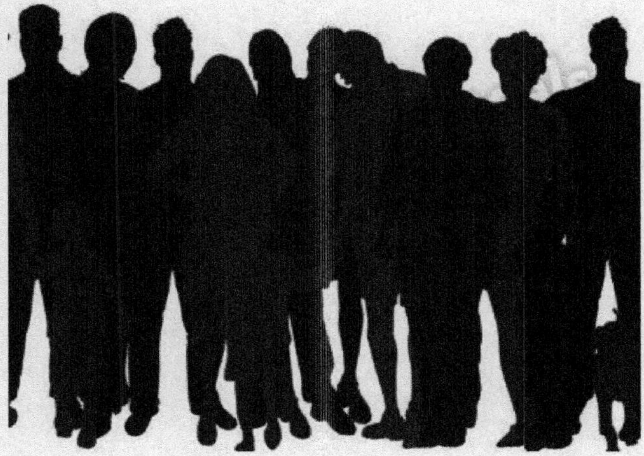

(Source - www.vetrinedecorate.it)

Chapter Two

The Hit-And-Run Business Mindset

"There is only one boss - the customer, and he can fire everybody in the company from the chairman on down, simply by spending his money somewhere else."
- Sam Walton

All the respondents during my research emphasised the fact that black businesses are entirely focused on making money as quickly as possible and nothing else matters. Consideration is not usually given to customer satisfaction that would encourage the customer to return for repeat business. I think it perfectly explains the underlying principle behind how most of our black businesses operate.

The respondents gave me different phrases to describe this business mindset. These are the best ones:

- 'Hit-and-run' businesses mindset
- 'Microwave-style' business concept
- 'Poverty-action' business owner

My favourite and most easily understood one is the phrase 'Hit-and-run' business mindset. I also received an African proverb that says it all.

Ghanian Proverb: Edidi daa ye sen Edidi kro. (English translation is - Eating a little every day is better than a one-off meal)

HOW TO IDENTIFY THE HIT-AND-RUN BUSINESS MINDSET.

These are black business owners who seem to care only about the money they can make in an instant, that day only without a care for future income and the longevity of the business. It is all about short-term thinking. The opposite of this is the 'Abundant-action' business owner, who thinks long term and not just about the profit they can make immediately.

To identify a 'Hit-and-run' mindset business owner, you would often notice the following characteristics:

- Demand a hundred percent upfront payment but refuse to complete the work.
- Offers poor quality of service and products.
- Unprofessional conduct.
- Exorbitant prices or overpriced products and services.
- Minimise cost to maximise profit to the detriment of the quality of the product and service provided.

The subsequent chapters will address all the above characteristics in great detail with some excellent true-life experiences to buttress the point. It appears these business owners are driven by the proverb:

'A bird in hand is worth ten in the bush'.

Hit-and-run businesses offer poor quality service and products to a customer who unhappily pays. The customer goes away with the decision to never patronise that business again, and even if they do not stop immediately, usually due to the unavailability of a better option, they do so eventually. Customers do not stop there; they tell everyone they know about their unpleasant experience, and that puts other potential customers off.

They say a satisfied customer will tell only a few people, but an unsatisfied customer will shout it out from the proverbial rooftop. In all of this, the business gets its money all the same- how else do we explain why this attitude to business persists?

To buttress this point, I will share these true-life experiences that I gathered from my research as narrated by the respondents.

MATTHEW'S STORY

Matthew is a Ugandan living in the UK. He needed to build a website for his business and, as his way of helping his people back home, he decided to award the project to a web designer based in his hometown of Uganda. This was a nice thing to do considering he could have easily paid a freelance web designer on most online platforms to do this for him quickly. Matthew was so happy to do his patriotic duty to his country that he paid for the work upfront.

He then spent over a year chasing the web designer to complete a job he had received payment for and his calls were either ignored or met with complaints that he was not patient enough. The web designer asked for more money for additional costs that Matthew sent, but that did not make a difference. Matthew's deadline for the website was still not met and the web designer also denied him access to the website when he asked for it. This is an excerpt from one of the frustrating WhatsApp conversations Matthew had with the web designer, which Matthew offered to share.

Matthew: *Hope you're well.*

Well done.

Web designer: *Hello*

Good evening, sir. Pardon the late reply. We are trying to move the website from Wix. Wix malfunctioned and we are trying to remove it and add word press changes.

The information is a lot and it's heavy. That is the updated. Kindly understand.

Matthew: *I need to talk to you. We have deadlines on the things that we do. Can you please send me the login details for my website. I need them ASAP. I need the login details please.*

Web designer: *Okay*

Matthew: *When?*

Really?? Do I have to beg you for the login details for my website? This is getting too far.

Web designer: *Hello sir. Please be patient.*

The website is about to get done. Let me share details.

Matthew: *Solomon is there a reason why you are not sending me the login details for my website?*

Web designer: *Let me share them. Just don't temper with anything.*

Matthew eventually gave up on this Ugandan web designer when he stopped communicating. I must commend Matthew for his patience because not many can wait that long. Matthew ended up hiring a non-black web designer in England, and the work was completed in a few weeks. He never received a refund from the Ugandan web designer.

JOSIE'S STORY

Josie organised a night out for twenty of her friends at a popular Nigerian restaurant. The owners of the restaurant were her close friends, and since they had been asking her to bring them business, Josie assumed the service would be fantastic on the day, and that with such a large number of customers, that at least one of the owners or a restaurant manager would be present to ensure it was a successful event. Josie had spoken so highly of the restaurant, from the food to the music and general ambience.

Josie set up a WhatsApp group with the restaurant owners to coordinate the event. She even went as far as getting her friends to preorder their food and fifteen of them did that.

On the night of the event, Josie arrived at the restaurant to learn that the owners would not be there because one was away on vacation while the other was attending a church service on the opposite side of town. They did not inform Josie beforehand despite the fact she had spoken to one of them that morning.

There were two inexperienced waitresses available to serve Josie's table of twenty, other customers in the restaurant and online food orders.

Unsurprisingly, the night was a disaster. Some of Josie's friends waited three hours for their food to arrive, despite pre-ordering the food. Ironically, those who refused to pre-order their meals were served even quicker than those who preordered.

The ladies complained and who could blame them? Josie was asked repeatedly if that was the same restaurant she spoke so highly about and she was too embarrassed to defend the restaurant owners who could not be bothered to inform her they would be away on the day.

Josie and her friends loved to dance, and they took to the dance floor to at least make up for the poor service, but it was soon interrupted by a neighbour barging into the restaurant to demand that the music volume be turned down because such loud music was not allowed in that neighbourhood.

The ladies became fed up and left the restaurant with a vow never to return there. These twenty angry customers spread the word. They could have been twenty satisfied customers who went away and came back with their friends and families, resulting in multiple group bookings and increased repeat business for that restaurant.

DAMAGE CONTROL

"The true test of a business's customer service fitness is not when things are going right- but rather what is done when things go wrong"

-Steve Ferrante

"7 out of 10 complaining customers will do business with you again if you resolve the complaint in their favour. If you resolve the complaint on the spot, 95% will do business with you again."

- (Source: www.slideplayer.com)

The owners apologised profusely to Josie after the event. They asked her to bring her friends back so they could be compensated for the terrible experience they had at the restaurant. They offered a fifty percent discount on the food and a free bottle of Prosecco. Josie liked that and tried to encourage her displeased friends to come for a repeat experience. Only ten of them were willing to give the restaurant another chance. The others said first impressions last forever and they did not see the point in going back there. When Josie was asked by the restaurant to send pre-orders, she refused to do so because it did not make any difference to the quality of service the last time.

A SECOND CHANCE

The second time Josie went back with her friends was an entirely different experience from the first time. She was keen to see if the restaurant could get it right this time.

They were welcomed warmly by the owners. They were served nice complimentary nibbles (a plate each) while their food was being prepared. The food was not delayed this time., and they enjoyed the food and free bottle of chilled Prosecco. The DJ played great music and it was uninterrupted this time. The owners apologised profusely for the disappointment and poor service last time. They thanked the ladies for giving them a second chance. The ladies had a fantastic time and they all went away happy.

Although the ten ladies who came back had a good time and gave the restaurant a second chance, they confided in Josie that they did not trust the restaurant to provide that same good quality of service the next time they visited as it was only better because the owners were present. They also said they could not recommend the restaurant to friends and family because there was no guarantee they would enjoy the same experience.

The good news is that six of those ladies and Josie have remained regular customers at that restaurant and they have held many ladies' nights at the restaurant after that. This shows the importance of damage control. This restaurant made a lot of money from the party of twenty that dined at the restaurant on the day but lost potential repeat business and recommendations in the process.

HOW TO GET IT RIGHT

1. Manage Expectations and communicate - Always advise your customer of delivery timescales from the start. Never wait for them to ask before you inform them.
2. If the food order will be delayed for any reason, offer complimentary nibbles like other restaurants do (Asian and Turkish).
3. Train and empower your staff to provide good service every time, especially in your absence.
4. Ensure consistency in quality of service.
5. I guess the obvious conclusion is this - As a business, aim to treat your customers well every time, not only after they complained.

Chapter Three

The Copycat Business Mindset

"Sabonshiga da Bubun mudu" - (English translation is "New business starter with a big measuring cup").

The above is a Hausa (Northern Nigerian tribe) proverb that means if an ignorant new business starter uses the largest measuring cup to sell his grains he will soon be making a loss. He must do his market research to understand the right size of measuring cup to use before he goes into the business of selling anything.

This is the perfect quote to kick off my discourse on this topic. Many of the respondents to my interviews and questionnaires about black businesses believe a second main problem why most of our black businesses fail is because their owners started the business simply to copy an existing business that has been seen to be profitable.

"When a business launches a successful product or service, competitors may feel compelled to create something similar to keep up with the market. This strategy, however, does not always work."
(Source - www.forbes.com)

Not much effort is put into market research to find out what the business model is and why it is successful in the first place. What soft skills are essential for all business relations and for serving customers? An understanding of this would indicate the type of training required for the owner and the staff to ensure the success of that business.

There is absolutely nothing wrong with a copycat business because that is where many businesses get their startup ideas from. For example, mobile phones have been around for ages. We all remember the Nokia, Blackberry or Sagem phones. Today we have the top brands like Apple and Samsung dominating the mobile phones market and that is because they improved upon the original mobile phone ideas. Therefore, if you must do a copycat business or copy a business idea, you should aim to do it better than the original. Do not simply copy everything, both the good and the bad aspects of that business model because that is what our black businesses do. Not enough effort is spent on market research to understand how to succeed at that type of business before setting it up.

Let's take a look at the number one and most successful legitimate copycat business model in the world. It is called FRANCHISING.

> *"A franchise (or franchising) is a method of distributing products or services involving a franchisor, who establishes the brand's trademark or trade name and a business system, and a franchisee, who pays a royalty and often an initial fee for the right to do business under the franchisor's name and system.*
> *(Source - www.franchise.org)*

The brilliant thing about this is that the Franchisor provides all the training and knowledge (know-how) necessary for the Franchisee to provide those goods or services. This is all part of the contract because the franchisor wants to protect its brand. It is a win-win situation because the franchisee will be confident of his chances to maintain a profitable business. This gives the new business every chance of success.

Check out this list of some of the biggest and best-known franchisees in the world.

- *McDonald's*
- *KFC*
- *Burger King*
- *Marriot International*
- *Subway Restaurants*

- *(Nando's is a Franchise only in South Africa, New Zealand, and Australia but not in the UK.)*

(Source: www.franchisedirect.com)

It appears that the failure of many copycat businesses by black people is due to this ignorance on how to operate that business. All our community sees is how profitable it is for Mr A, therefore Mr B thinks he can do the exact same thing. Therefore, the business is here today and gone tomorrow. Some learn how to set it up but not how to run it which is the most important part of the process.

Churches in Africa are perhaps the most visible form of a copycat business. Although a church is not typically a business, (for example, in the UK, churches are registered as charities) in Africa they appear like businesses. We have two or three churches of the same denomination on almost every street in Nigeria and church members are spread thinly among the churches. How many people live on that street that requires those two or three churches? Do we need that many churches? Why can't these churches on the same street collaborate and work to develop one church in that area? I must point out the fact that only the Pentecostal churches do this. The more traditional churches like Catholic, Anglican, Baptist and Methodist churches do not practice this.

Everyone wants to be a pastor without knowing their 'true calling'. It looks like a one-man business with the pastor doing everything instead of delegating to people according to their spiritual strengths.

Let's look at some true-life experiences of a bad copycat black business.

A COPYCAT DJ

In a city in the United Kingdom, there was a very good DJ. He was well-known in the area for providing the best music and knew how to please a crowd. He did this for over a decade. One day another black guy moved into the area and noticed that DJ 1 was making a lot of money from the business. Let's call him DJ 2.

DJ 2 decided he was good at spinning a deck so that meant he could be a DJ, too. He started his own DJ business. The first gig he got was to provide music at a fiftieth birthday party. DJ 2 did not understand the age group and the right music to please them and played Spice Girls songs, which was the wrong type of music to play for that age group. After that, no one booked DJ 2 for a gig anymore and he got upset about it and blamed the community for not supporting him when the problem was his lack of understanding of a business he tried to copy.

Hairdressers are another good example of copycat businesses. Sometimes, I think any black woman who knows how to braid hair thinks that automatically qualifies them as a hairdresser. They rent a seat in a salon and start to serve customers. Many display a complete lack of understanding of the business operations and customer service or customer satisfaction. The same goes for black tailors. Just because you learnt how to sew a few dresses is not a qualification to run a tailoring business. A lot more is required to make it a successful business. We will cover the topic of poor-quality products and services in the next chapter.

The final example of copycat businesses is in the IT consulting profession. I have sat in on several training sessions and spoken with many of my IT professional colleagues. Everyone wants to be a PMO Analyst, project manager, Business Analyst or scrum master, and the driver or motivation is the remuneration (daily rate). We know these jobs pay very good wages and most black professionals in this industry are doing mainly these three types of jobs. Not much thought is given to whether this is the right job for them or whether they actually like doing that job. Do they possess the soft skills required for these roles? Those skills determine your ability to succeed in such jobs, but all they care about is the money.

A lot of focus is on the paper qualifications (Prince 2/ Business Analysis certifications, Agile project management, scrum master, etc). It is easy to get these certifications, but the experience and soft skills required (interpersonal skills, communication skills, conflict resolution skills, team spirit, etc) could be a deal breaker here. Some go into these jobs blindly as 'cowboys'- a term used to describe someone who claims they have work experience that they do not. Many fall by the wayside because they are fired from the job or unable to get a job because they cannot lie or blag their way through the interview process. It takes some level of self-confidence and boldness to accomplish that.

Many become frustrated and end up finding a different career path. I must admit many succeed at it too. My point is do not just copy a business model because your friends and those in your black community are doing that job. Be patient, do your research and be sure it is the right role for you, then do it properly. Otherwise, you will be wasting a lot of money on training that may not be required for the career you end up with.

HOW TO GET IT RIGHT

There is nothing wrong with copying a successful business as long as you do it properly and strive to make yours even better than the one you copied. These tips may help.

1. Maintain your originality.
2. You may have short-term success copying, but if you are a leader in the true sense of the word, be original. The only way you'll have a good chance of success is to make a better product and service than the original. Most importantly, reputation is everything. If you are labelled a copycat in any shape or form, you may lose

credibility, which could cause irreparable damage to your business.

3. Target customer needs.
4. Prioritize solving pain points.
5. Stay focused on why people use your service.
6. Personalize the offering for your target audience.
7. Understand the reasons behind the original product's success.
8. Find the unmet gap.

(Source-www.forbes.com)

This is where a thorough market research comes in. It should be done at the beginning of the business as a bare minimum. However, if that did not happen, it can be done after startup. This is why a business plan is highly recommended at the start and should be revisited regularly and tweaked for necessary updates and improvements.

Chapter Four

Quality Of Goods & Services

"It takes 20 years to build a reputation and five minutes to ruin it. If you think about it, you will do things differently".
-Warren Buffet (CEO of Berkshire Hathaway)

There was a time when a GOOD NAME was better than RICHES, but today most black businesses do not seem to care about their business reputation. Instead, they care about the RICHES.

This is probably the most important or significant chapter in this book because it is perhaps the topic that impacts our daily lives the most. My research from interviewing black consumers worldwide revealed a unanimous statement from the respondents; black businesses do not understand CUSTOMER SERVICE. The quality of service was described as ABYSMAL because they do not know how to delight customers or go the extra mile to exceed a customer's expectations.

- Why is that?
- Is it that they cannot be bothered to make the effort?
- Is it a belief that they have a good product or service, so the customer will definitely come back? (e.g the only black salon in the neighbourhood).

For a detailed analysis of this issue, I will focus on the key business sectors to highlight their peculiarities.

BLACK-OWNED RESTAURANTS

The consensus from the respondents is that our restaurants are known for very slow or delayed service. You can find yourself waiting for up to two hours for your order. No one offers any explanation for the delay or how long it will take. In chapter two, we learnt of Josie's experience and how long it took her and her friends to get served, despite preordering the food weeks in advance.

There is a restaurant in Southeast London known for their amazing food. They are the best place for seafood okra soup and garnished beef. They are also the worst for food delays. One respondent mentioned ordering his food days in advance for pick up but when he arrived, he still had to wait for hours for the food to be served. He has stopped eating at that restaurant unless he has plenty of time to waste, which he does not. Why can't this restaurant get the service standards, right?

The consistency in the quality of the food was another issue. One day the food is great and the next time, it is not so tasty. You never know what you will get when you order food at some black restaurants. I believe the reason for this problem is that our community is used to cooking food without written recipes. Therefore, the measurement of the ingredients is never the same each time we cook. Sometimes the salt or spices is just right, but at other times they are either too much or too little. The result is inconsistency in the taste of the food each time. One could argue that a good chef is capable of maintaining the same quality and consistency in the taste of the food every time but even that is impossible to achieve.

There is also the problem of a high turnover of chefs in black-owned restaurants. They do not seem to last long and are replaced frequently. The chefs are usually not well trained in the art of cooking for a restaurant; they are usually people who just know how to cook well who are hired to do the job.

My research also revealed something I never knew existed. The term 'CARIBBEAN-SERVICE' is used to describe the hostile customer service you receive at Caribbean restaurants. The consensus was that you meet very rude and unfriendly staff at these restaurants. The customer is seen as a disturbance instead of someone that came to do you the favour of buying your products. When you walk into a Caribbean restaurant, you are not greeted with a smile or a friendly:

"Hello, what would you like today?"

Instead, what you hear is this unwelcome question:

"What you want?" with a big frown or scowl.

If I walk into a restaurant and the customer service staff or waitress said that to me, I will turn around and walk away. It is said that this is why you do not find long queues at Caribbean restaurants.

That being said, I visited a couple of Caribbean restaurants and received very nice and friendly service from one of them and a frosty one from the other. So, I guess there is some hope yet. That is also why we should not generalise.

Black-owned restaurants open much later and close earlier than most non-black-owned restaurants. This does not only occur in the restaurant business because most black businesses do this and that is why there is a school of thought that we are too lazy to make money. We shall explore this later in this book.

Inappropriate pricing system and raising prices exorbitantly without notifying customers in advance was also an issue highlighted by many of my respondents and it will be addressed in later chapters.

HOW TO GET IT RIGHT

1. Research! Research! Research how to operate a restaurant business. Never go into any business blindly unless you want the business to fail. Even successful restauranteurs with decades of experience still carry out market research for continuous improvement. The black community needs to start doing this for all our businesses.
2. Document your best recipes for consistency. This way, the restaurant can maintain the consistency of the food quality even when they change chefs.

3. Communicate! Communicate! Communicate! I cannot overemphasise this enough. Inform the customers how long it will take so they are forewarned and can decide if they are prepared to wait or not. It is called MANAGING EXPECTATIONS.
4. Offer complimentary nibbles while customers wait for the food. Non-black restaurants do this very well. Turkish restaurants offer a small basket of soft warm bread and dips. Chinese restaurants offer prawn crackers while English restaurants offer small bread rolls with butter. Luckily for our black culture, we are spoilt for choice. We have roasted peanuts, chin-chin (small, crunchy cookie-like bites of fried dough), plantain chips, etc. There are so many great brands of these products in the market that can be purchased for a little amount and be served to customers. I gave this advice to a friend who owns a black restaurant, and he has implemented this to the delight of their customers.
5. Parboil or precook large quantities of the ingredients that usually take longer to cook. Fish, meat, poultry, beans and freeze them. Microwave to defrost or place in a boiling soup pot and it will defrost quickly. These are necessary time-saving measures that would make a difference.

BLACK-OWNED AFRICAN GROCERY STORES

We want to spend less money on good quality products and great customer service. This is what we want, but hardly what we get.

One consensus from most respondents was the poor customer service at the counter. Most times the cashier is on the phone when you walk in, and they remain on the phone throughout your shopping experience, making it difficult for you to ask questions.

Some sell expired food items or inedible food to you, like a piece of yam that is rotting on the inside but looks good on the outside. That is why most customers now ask retailers to cut the tuber of yam in the middle to ensure it is edible before they pay for it. I know the rotting yam is by no means the fault of the retailer, but selling it as soon as possible before it starts to rot would be my suggestion. Why not sell it at a reduced price when it is no longer as fresh as it used to be?

Unfortunately, yam does not come with an expiry date and so is plantain. With plantain, there is no excuse because you can see clearly from the exterior colour that it is becoming overripe and starting to rot. What any sensible food retailer would do in that situation is to sell that plantain off at a reduced price, but not our black retailers. They insist on selling it off at the same price which no customers would buy and they end up chucking the plantain away.

Another thing some respondents complained about is that they do not bother taking any bad or inedible food items back to the store for fear of being insulted. The food retailers deny that the food was bad when you bought it from them and blame you for it even if you took it back the same day. Some call you an "enemy of progress" that wants to tarnish their image and spoil their business. They then refuse to replace that food item.

Black customers see it as too much trouble to return anything or ask for a refund. A replacement is the best you can hope for and which you probably won't get.

Black customers return expired or inedible food items to non-black owned stores but are reluctant to do so when it is a black business. Is this out of loyalty not to cause problems for the black business? Are they really helping the black business by not giving that necessary feedback?

I bought poultry from an Asian retailer once and it smelled awful when I brought it out of my bag to cook. I took it back the next day and I received an apology and a prompt replacement with an extra piece of chicken drumstick. Just compare this to the experience at black food retailers.

African food retailers tend to sell everything instead of focusing on just food. They sell Afro hair products and African clothing, and you may find the yam tubers tucked behind the clothes. It would be nice if they focused on just food. We will explore the reason behind this in later chapters.

BLACK CATERERS

The mission statement or modus operandi of black caterers seems to be to minimise cost and maximise profit. What we want is a caterer who delivers exactly what she shows us on the menu and in her quotation. When we have surplus food and drinks at our parties, the caterer should ask us what we want to do with the leftovers, since we paid for them already.

The consensus from the respondents about black caterers is that they cut corners or try to maximise their profit by giving you less than what you paid for. What you pay for is not what you get.

They usually leave a few things out, and this may be easy for them to do because it is usually quite busy at an event and no one checks the number of crates of drinks, pieces of meat or plates of food served. It is either there is more than enough food for the guests or there isn't enough food. It is usually the latter.

Another pain point is their late arrival to the venue. They never turn up early and you find yourself frantically calling them to know why they are delayed. Some have been known to serve cold food instead of hot food because they turned up late and did not have adequate set-up time.

Since the caterer's strategy is always to minimise cost and maximise profit, the taste and quality of the food is usually below expectation. I have witnessed a cake being delivered almost at the end of a kid's birthday party. The mother wept at the disappointment.

HOW TO GET IT RIGHT

1. I cannot emphasise this enough. Communication is everything. Inform the clients if you are running late to manage their expectations.
2. Remember if you do all the negative things mentioned above, no customer would recommend you.
3. Anyone who tries the poor quality of your food the first time will not return.
4. What happens to party leftover food and drinks is a decision for your client. Please ask their permission before taking anything away.
5. An event in a hired hall has only a limited time to use that space. Consider that and arrive even earlier to set up and be able to vacate the premises at the right time.

BLACK HAIRDRESSERS/ BEAUTICIANS/BARBERS

Hairdressers are the bane of a black woman's existence. This is not news because our hair is high maintenance. It needs regular treatment, plaiting and styling. Whether you prefer braids with extensions, weave-on extensions, corn rows, crochet, locks, twists, relax and perm, texturing, etc. The list is endless and this is by no means exhaustive.

All of these hairstyles are not cheap, and neither are the materials you have to buy to have them done. As an example, there is a Brazilian weave extension that costs as much as a hundred or thousand pounds.

What we want is a hairdresser or barber who is ready to do our hair at the time we both agreed on to avoid indefinite waiting periods; clean and tidy hair salons; the right price; communication if they are running late on their way to your house to plait your hair. One respondent told me about her experience of booking appointments with her regular black barber and on two occasions, he travelled out of town without informing her. She found out about his unavailability when she arrived at the salon which was closed. When she called him, he did not apologise to her. He simply said he forgot to inform her. This is clearly a business owner who does not value his customers.

We have three categories of hairdressers. There are the 'African aunties', the generation Z young black hairdressers and beauticians, and lastly, the high-end and well-established hairdressing salons.

AFRICAN AUNTIE HAIRDRESSER - PROS /CONS

- Not well educated. Age varies.
- Price is cheaper (e.g. £50 for braids).
- Do not charge a deposit for a booking or charge for lateness.
- No appointment booking system. Often double-books and indefinite waiting periods (Even longer when the customer is a kid).
- Offers limited range of hair services and no beauty services (e.g do not fix false eyelashes).
- More flexible and would do the corn row and pre-pull the weave for braids)
- Not tech savvy
- Home salon premises/ business salon premises are often overcrowded and untidy.
- Always there when they give you an appointment.

This category of hairdressers is quite exasperating because of the unprofessionalism and a complete lack of business acumen. They never say no to a booking or that they are fully booked for the day. This is how the conversation often goes:

Customer: Hello Bukky!

Hairdresser: Good afternoon, Sister!

Customer: I would like to braid my hair. When are you available?

Hairdresser: When do you want to come?

Customer: On Saturday. What time are you available?

Hairdresser: Just come! Come anytime I will do it for you.

Customer: No, no, give me a specific time o! I don't want to come there and wait for hours.

Hairdresser: Ok, let me check.

(After a brief pause)

Hairdresser: Can you come at 2 o'clock?

Customer: Yes, I can. Thank you, Bukky.

Hairdresser: Yes ma.

Customer: Please I don't want to come and wait o! I hope this 2 pm will not become 4 pm like last time?

Hairdresser: Haba! No ma. I will finish my last customer before that 2 o'clock, ma.

Customer: Ok, that's good. See you on Saturday then.

Hairdresser: Ok ma.

When Saturday arrives, the hairdresser is double booked, and you often meet one or two other customers waiting before you. You either have to stay or walk away to find another hairdresser which is often difficult to find on the same day as most hairdressers would be booked as well. Even if you do, it may require travelling to another location. So you end up staying and wasting the rest of your day at the salon.

The reason for this double or triple booking is obviously greed and an attempt to make as much money as possible. One collapsed from exhaustion as a result of being on her feet the whole day. They do not take a well-deserved and necessary lunch break. Instead, they eat finger food and drink a bottle of malt vitality drinks whilst making hair. Who knows how many food crumbs will make their way into the customer's hair?

A friend of mine had a 9 am appointment but did not leave the salon until 5:30 pm because the hairdresser had to stop several times to attend to other customers. Shocking, isn't it? The customer is caught between a rock and a hard place because she cannot leave with her hair half-done. This is the usual nightmare.

Of course, as an adult, you can make a fuss and insist that your hair must be completed. Imagine if the customer was a kid or teenager. The hairdressers take them for granted and treat kids much worse, especially if the parent is not present. Most parents would drop their kids with the hairdresser and come back in an hour or two to pick them up. As soon as the parent departs, the kid's hair will be abandoned by the hairdresser so she can serve someone else's, usually an adult customer. After an hour, they return to plaiting the kid's hair. This has happened to my daughter several times when I drop her off at the salon to have her hair done. Many of my women friends told me their daughters DO NOT WANT AFRICAN AUNTIES TO DO THEIR HAIR because they shut them down if they complain. They hate going to African aunties and I believe them because my teenage daughter said the same thing.

Some women resorted to inviting the hairdresser to their home as a way of mitigating this time wasting, but on one occasion a hairdresser arrived five hours late without a call or text to explain that she would be late. She ignored all calls and texts until she was on the bus to the location. Her explanation was a sob story about childcare problems she had to resolve before leaving home. It was revealed later that she went somewhere else to do another quick hairdressing job and ended up arriving five hours late.

Why did she not call to say she would be late?

Why did she not reschedule?

No, they never reschedule for fear of losing the money to be made for the day. The customer suffers because that five hours could have been spent doing something or running a few errands. Instead, the customer had to stay at home waiting because she believed the hairdresser may turn up anytime, which of course she did not until five hours later than scheduled.

Another option is to go pick up the hairdresser from their home and bring them down to yours, especially if they do not have a car. I did this on a few occasions, and it was perfect. No delays, no messing around. This works if the hairdresser does not live far away from your home or does not have a salon where she works.

All this palaver just to fix your hair or your daughters' hair? I must mention that this only works for braids. If you have to relax, wash and perm your hair, it cannot be done in your home. You would have to go to a hairdressing salon for that.

I gave up my lovely short curly hair which always got me great compliments because the hairdresser hurt my scalp every time, she tonged my hair. Yes, I know the hair is short, but I expect the hairdresser to be cautious and have the skill to do this without hurting my scalp in the process. Whenever I winced in pain and asked the hairdresser to be careful with the tong, I always heard the same response:

'It is not my fault, your hair is too short!'

In other words, it is my fault for trying to maintain a short hairstyle. How about trying not to cause the customer pain or bodily harm?

Eventually, I found a hairdresser who had the skill and knowledge to tong short hair by simply placing a small comb between the tong and my scalp to prevent damaging my scalp. I was so glad to find her and she was my hairdresser for many years until she moved to a different town. It was too far away for me to travel to frequently as required because short, relaxed hair is even more high maintenance. I had to make the tough decision to change to a longer hairstyle after that.

GENERATION Z HAIRDRESSERS

- Quite young - from age 15.
- Educated/students and tech savvy.
- Appointment booking system on instagram.
- Take a £20 non-refundable deposit via a link on Instagram. This is okay in case a customer cancels the appointment. However, when the hairdresser cancels your booking, they do not refund that deposit to the annoyance of their customers. (Sometimes, they go on holiday without cancelling an appointment and foolishly post the photos on social media for all to see).
- Charges for lateness.
- Home/ salon premises nicely furnished, clean and tidy.
- Inflexible - will not do corn rows for weaves or pre-pull/ straighten extensions.
- Offers more comprehensive hair and beauty services to include eyelash fixing and waxing services.
- Price is higher (£90 for braids and £185 for wigs/frontal. eyelash fixing- £50 - £90).

This category is clearly out of control, and it may be down to their young age and lack of experience and business acumen. Should a fifteen-year-old be running a business? One respondent told me about angry customers turning up at the home of some of these hairdressers to beat them up and it is usually for taking money and not providing the service. I think parents of these young hairdressers should step in and provide the necessary support and guidance needed here.

When these black Instagram hairdressers receive bad reviews on TikTok or Instagram, they do not take them on board and make necessary improvements. Instead, they simply change their profiles and rebrand.

This category is mainly patronised by teenagers and young women.

BLACK HIGH-END HAIR BEAUTY SALONS

This business category will not be complete if I do not mention the luxury hair salons. They provide exceptional service consistently. They are characterised by the following:

- Highly experienced staff
- High-Quality products and equipment
- Variety of services beyond hair, such as massages and skin and body treatments
- Offer snacks and drinks (even champagne)
- Provides a luxury experience in a great location and a stress-free and comfortable environment where you will find very high-quality furniture and relaxing music.

- Excellent customer service every time
- Being up to date on the latest trends, styles and products
- Attracts affluent clients.
- Mostly profitable: They make a lot of money because they offer the best and can justifiably charge a lot for it.

I think these high-end salons are the best institutions or establishments to do an apprenticeship if you want to run a business in the hair and beauty industry. The reason is clear. This is where you can learn best practices and excellent skills.

A respondent told me how her daughter graduated from university and did an apprenticeship in one of these salons. After her apprenticeship, she became a stylist for models and actresses. She currently travels all over the world because she is hired by Marc Jacobs, Valentino, Christian Dior, etc. for their fashion shows to style their models.

HOW TO GET IT RIGHT

1. Hairdressers should learn wherever they have skill gaps to improve the service they offer.
2. Call if you are running late. We don't mind as long as you tell us in good time.
3. Stop the greed by double/triple booking people even with thirty minutes apart because we know you cannot finish any black hairstyle in thirty minutes.

4. Maintain a calendar or schedule for your appointments and take breaks during the day so you don't collapse.
5. Get your pricing correct and appropriate. Mums are learning how to fix hair for themselves and their children so they can avoid hairdressers. They're relaxing and braiding their own hair. Most of my friends do, including myself. Saves us a lot of money and time.

THE BLACK TAILOR/DRESSMAKER

This is another category of black business owners that could drive you up the wall with their level of poor-quality products and services. It is exasperating. The desire to make quick money by black businesses is the main reason why so many bad decisions are made, and the customers are treated unfairly.

The African community love to wear prints, popularly known as Ankara for special occasions. It is a made-to-order outfit and the best part is that you can choose the fabric and style you want, and the tailor will make it to your exact specifications.

In Africa, there are so many tailors in the community, and you are spoiled for choice. However, as a black person living in the West, it is a nightmare.

First and foremost, there are not enough skilled tailors available. There are those who briefly learnt how to make dresses and decided to offer their services. I have encountered many of these unskilled tailors, although I did not know at the time. The tailors took a deposit before sewing and ended up charging me exorbitant amounts for styles they could not replicate, leaving me with damaged fabrics in terrible outfit that could not be worn. These fabrics cost money and at the end of the day, I had no dresses to show for it, just money wasted. They also did not give refunds.

In one such experience, I wore the dress because I thought it was manageable and also because I liked the fabric so much. At that point, I did not know that the tailor was still learning how to sew. A friend took one look at me and asked who made the dress. When I told her, she was astonished. She informed me the woman was not a tailor yet, but one in training.

ETHEL'S STORY

A respondent complained that her tailor never says no to a new order. Let's call the respondent Ethel for this narrative. Her dressmaker accepts fabrics, receives part payment, and promises to deliver by the agreed date, but when that date arrived, the dress is not ready. When she calls the tailor, she either refuses to take her call or ignores her messages.

On one occasion, the tailor asked Ethel to come pick up the dress and when she turned up at the gate, the tailor refused to let her in. She called her mobile number repeatedly but the tailor ignored the call. After knocking repeatedly, Ethel decided to sit in her car and wait until the gate was opened.

An hour later, someone emerged from the gate, and she was able to get in. The tailor was forced to open her door at that point. She apologised that she overslept and did not hear the doorbell or her phone ringing. Ethel knew she was lying but did not bother to argue about that when there was a more important thing - her dress.

To Ethel's surprise, the tailor's living room was filled with Ankara fabrics strewn everywhere. The tailor had to dig under the pile to fish out Ethel's unfinished fabrics. Ethel could not take the fabric away in that state and was too upset to say much. She managed to ask the burning question I am sure many would like an answer to:

Ethel: Why do you take so many orders when you know you cannot complete them at the required time?

Tailor: Ehn! How can I say no to business? Did I come to the UK to look at London Bridge? Sister, how can you say that? Abomination!

Customer: So, how will you satisfy all these customers? Look at these fabrics. Do you have any staff?

Tailor: Why do I need a staff? What if they spoil a customer's cloth? No o! Olorun maje! (Meaning God forbid it in Yoruba)

Customer: I needed this dress for aso ebi and now you have disappointed me.

Tailor: I am sorry, sister. I will finish it today and bring it to your house.

Customer: I will believe it when I see it.

Ethel left and wondered why her friend introduced her to such a terrible and unprofessional dressmaker. Unsurprisingly, the dressmaker never showed up that day with her dress. It took another month before that dress was made.

Ethel asked her apologetic friend who regretted introducing the dressmaker to her to collect the clothes on her behalf because she could not bear to do business with the dressmaker anymore. Ethel stopped making Ankara dresses and resorted to buying ready-made ones instead. She also avoided taking part in aso ebi for occasions.

Ethel's story is not a unique one. Many black dressmakers are like this. They never say no to new orders even when they know they cannot meet the delivery deadline.

BUSINESS PREMISES

The quality of business premises is part of the quality of services provided to customers, so this needs to be addressed too.

Most Black businesses do not have appropriate business premises and the facilities are often ghastly. I received many examples of that. Black restaurants with smelly toilets, etc. (Some respondents told me that a dirty toilet is a deal breaker for them. They check the toilets before sitting down for a meal and if it is dirty, they walk out immediately).

The premises often lack parking facilities; there are always tight spaces you cannot easily drive to or pack your car.

The black business restaurants often offer dining and dancing services with a DJ at weekends to provide the music. The restaurant becomes a nightclub at weekends to please black customers because we like to dance and have a good time.

However, the problem is that a dancing area is not created in the restaurant for the comfort of the dancing customers. Instead, they have to dance in between dining customers. I have experienced this many times and it is not a good experience.

Home Hair Salon - Some hairdressers provide their services from their homes. Generation Z hairdressers often have beautiful premises and facilities where they conduct their business. The same cannot be said for most of African Aunties hairdressers.

Our teenagers and young girls refuse to have their hair done by African aunties especially when it is done in the hairdresser's home. This is because the house would be messy with hair all over the floor and wet clothes spread on the radiator to dry.

HOW TO GET IT RIGHT

1. Not every black restaurant should provide a DJ and dancing as part of their service unless they have adequate space for it.
2. Ensure the toilets are kept clean and well fragranced

considering the amount of human traffic going in and out. If other non-black business premises can provide this, then we can do the same.

BLACK BUILDERS

The pain point is how long it takes for the work to be completed. They often abandon the work midway.

TESSY'S STORY

Tessy works in a Local Authority in the UK. She had the opportunity to hire a builder and electrician to do repairs on commercial properties. The rate was eight hundred pounds a day. The black builder and electrician started the job and disappeared after two days without completing the work. Tessy had to hire a non-black builder to come in and complete the job over a few days and he made even more money for it.

BLACK SOLICITORS / LAWYERS

The general impression is that they tend to prolong your case so they can continue to make more money off you. They offer wrong advice to prolong a case that could have been resolved much quicker.

If you are an educated person, look out for when you are being given the wrong advice. Especially with immigration lawyers who ask for payment before they do anything on the case.

Chapter Five

Unprofessionalism

"A customer is the most important visitor on our premises. He is not dependent on us. We are dependent on him/her. He is not an interruption in our work. He is the purpose of it. He is not an outsider in our business. He is part of it. We are not doing him a favour by serving him. He is doing us a favour by giving us an opportunity to do so".

-Mahatma Gandhi

There is a general belief that black businesses have a nonchalant attitude towards professionalism. They do not seem to care about it when you complain to them; they simply shrug it off. Unprofessionalism was the biggest turn off according to most of the respondents. Let's find out why.

'BLACK-MAN-TIME' - 'AFRICAN-TIME'

This is perhaps the most well-known problem we have in our community because it is tardiness that is displayed by most black people worldwide. It is our inability to be punctual to appointments or events.

We are known to turn up over an hour late to appointments. Our events are known to begin over an hour or two behind schedule. As a race, we laugh and make jokes about this and even gave it a name. It is now popularly known as 'Black-man-time' or 'African time'. This is not funny, and we should take it seriously, but instead, it has become the norm. It is safe to say that we have NORMALISED THE ABNORMAL; we even turn up late to online events taking place virtually on video conferencing tools like Zoom.

If you turn up at the scheduled time for an event or complain about lateness, this is the response you will get:

"Why are you behaving like a white person?"

Or as Nigerians put it in Pidgin English,

"Why you dey behave like Oyinbo person".

However, we do manage to turn up on time when we are in paid employment. Is that because we know what is at stake? Or because we know it would impact our job and income? That explains why we never go late to job interviews too.

The focus here is on business practices. Black business owners turn up late for appointments all the time. Caterers deliver food shortly before the end of a party. I saw a mum weeping at her kid's birthday party because the cake she ordered was not delivered until about thirty minutes to the end of the party, which took place in a hired venue and had to end at the scheduled time.

However, paid events and concerts are the worst. I have attended Gala nights and comedy shows that began two hours after the scheduled start time. Surprisingly, the organisers and Master of ceremony (MC) did not apologise for the late start. How unprofessional is that? How can an MC, the host of an event, turn up late to the event?

Everyone has accepted it as the norm. I hear my friends and family boast that they never arrive at an event at the scheduled time because they know the venue would be empty at that time and the event would start late anyway. My answer is always this:

> *"How will the venue ever fill up if everyone has this same mindset about turning up late?"*

I have been late to events myself but I make every effort not to. One thing I ensure to do is to inform the host or client that I am running late and apologise in the process.

HOW TO GET IT RIGHT

1. Turning up late is unprofessional and should be avoided at all cost.
2. Once again, COMMUNICATE! COMMUNICATE! Call ahead to apologise if you are running late. Your client would appreciate it and respect you for that. It is unprofessional not to. Remember you could lose a business for that reason.

3. For caterers, please inform your client if you cannot deliver the order at the right time and give them the option to pick it up themselves. These days, you can pay for Uber to deliver the food to the venue. I often pick up my order of food and drinks from the caterer instead of waiting for it to be delivered. That is what I do. Although I must admit this would depend largely on the size of the order. This could work for small orders, especially for cakes but maybe not for large orders.

INABILITY TO ACCEPT FEEDBACK

It is said that Black businesses do not take feedback well. They see it as criticism instead of a chance to fix the problems. I have heard black business owners complain that negative feedback is an attempt to destroy their business. This has happened to me and my friends; the owners insult you for suggesting improvements.

Female customers at a restaurant were told they are only complaining because they are women and that male customers do not complain; therefore, the women were the problem.

In the previous chapter, we learnt how black-owned African grocery stores argue and insult you if you return an inedible or rotting food item. Some respondents said they do not bother giving feedback anymore, because they have learnt to lower their expectations. Are they really helping the black business by not giving that necessary feedback?

A wise business owner considers feedback a gift , and will use it to make the necessary improvements to satisfy more customers. An unwise business owner will take it as criticism and ignore it. They usually end up losing more customers and eventually stop turning a profit and shut the business down. It is obvious what the best cause of action is.

If you're a black business, the way you chose to react to this book will determine where you sit on either side of the spectrum. Feedback is a gift. Please see this book as such.

UNWISE BUSINESS OWNER

When the Generation Z Instagram black hairdressers receive bad reviews on TikTok or Instagram, they do not take it on board and make the necessary improvements. Instead they simply change their profile and rebrand. They eventually make the same mistakes, because they are the same people doing the exact same thing. How long will they keep changing their social media handles?

WISE BUSINESS OWNER

There is a very nice and black-owned African grocery store in my neighbourhood. I have had to return an awful-tasting bottle of peanuts and rotten yam to her store and she replaced them immediately with an apology. Hmmmm.... is this down to her education?

I told her once that the moin-moin (beans pudding) that I bought from her did not taste the same after freezing it and she took my feedback on board, complained to the supplier and soon after there was such a great improvement in that moin-moin that I have recommended it to my friends, which means more business for the grocery store. That is how you do it.

MAKING EXCUSES ABOUT PERSONAL PROBLEMS

Most Black businesses behave like they are doing you a favour instead of the other way around. Once they get paid in full, they lose interest in providing the services. You almost have to beg to get the work done. That is how many of my respondents described it. Imagine pushing or asking someone to do a job they have already been paid for.

It is at this point that they resort to making excuses using personal and domestic reasons for the delay in completing the work. Ponder these examples:

ANDREW'S STORY

Andrew is a lawyer who relocated from Nigeria to Canada. A dear friend of his asked him to recommend one of his lawyer colleagues in Nigeria to handle a probate case. He recommended the only probate lawyer he knew, who was not well known to Andrew. The lawyer asked for a high legal fee, which the client paid in full.

For two months the client was chasing the lawyer to carry out the work he has been paid to do and all the probate lawyer did was complain about his heavy workload with rich clients and the fuel scarcity, lack of electricity and the terrible economy in Nigeria.

Dear readers, I know what you are thinking. Fuel scarcity and electricity outages were existing problems in the country before the case was assigned to him. How could that be reason he failed to execute the job? The lawyer made so many promises to deliver the job but never kept his promise. It was always ' I WILL FILE IT NEXT WEEK'.

Sadly, that NEXT WEEK came and went several times. The client could not believe anything the lawyer said. The case was due in court in less than two weeks, so the client was frantic. All trust was now eroded and as a last resort, the fed-up client went back to Andrew for intervention. It took several calls from Andrew and a threat to withdraw another case from him and never recommend the probate lawyer to anyone else that finally made him do the job he was paid for.

The lawyer did such a terrible job that Andrew had to spend hours on a Zoom session to coach the probate lawyer on how best to handle the case. That lawyer lost repeat business and referral business from Andrew and the new client in London. He made some good money on that case, but did not make any more from those clients.

DIPO'S STORY

Dipo's immigration lawyer travelled to Nigeria on a business trip when he was scheduled to represent Dipo at a court hearing. He did not inform Dipo beforehand. He avoided all the calls and waited until the last minute to inform Dipo that he was abroad. How could he be in Nigeria when he had a case in Birmingham UK? Perplexing, isn't it? Why do black businesses find it so difficult to communicate?

Considering this lawyer had a client like Dipo, who was stressed and anxious about the outcome of the court hearing and needed reassurance more than anything, he sent another lawyer from the firm to take his place and Dipo only found out that day by text message.

Of course, they messed up the case because the new lawyer was not quite familiar with the case and did not have adequate time to discuss the case before the court hearing. Dipo eventually fired his lawyer and found another lawyer who valued his patronage.

The respondents want to know why Black businesses think it is okay to complain to clients and customers about their personal and domestic problems. They use these problems as excuses and expect us to understand because we are fellow black people, or in this case, fellow Nigerians. Why can't they see how unprofessional it is to do that?

When I deal with non-black businesses, they simply do the job. They do not bother you with their personal problems because it has nothing to do with the client. If the delivery of a product or service will be delayed, they will apologise and inform you in advance.

They do not leave it until the last minute and expect you to accept it because you are a FELLOW BLACK PERSON. This leads me to the next topic.

TAKING BLACK CUSTOMERS FOR GRANTED

Black businesses should treat all customers the same way, no matter the colour of their skin. What the black community has observed is that black businesses treat non-black customers much better than fellow black customers. They treat them with deference. This is a clear case of an inferiority complex.

Is this mental slavery? An attitude of servitude to the white man? Is this what Bob Marley meant in his song when he sang "Emancipate yourself from mental slavery?"

This is the saddest thing I learned in my research. Black people in the diaspora have to deal with all forms of racism and discrimination from non-black people. We have all read and watched images and videos of police brutality in the news and on social media. The most high-profile ones are George Floyd in the USA, Stephen Lawrence in the UK (not police brutality) and Nahel Merzouk in France.

This proves that black people are already been persecuted in so many ways and living such difficult lives. Therefore, why do we not show the same love and respect to our fellow black people.?

Black businesses are outward-looking because they treat other ethnic groups better than their fellow black customers. They tend to devalue their black customers. Most of the respondents emphasised this issue and gave numerous examples.

Some put it down to the colonial mindset and it is more prevalent in Africa. If a non-black customer walks into a restaurant, store or any other business premises, the customer service staff would hurry towards the non-black customers to serve them first. They address them as "Sir/Madam" and ignore the black customers entirely until the non-black customer is served. The professional thing to do is to serve the customers in the order of arrival, based on who came in first.

MABEL'S STORY

"I was queuing up to process NIN in Lagos, Nigeria. As soon as a couple of Lebanese customers showed up, the team were falling over themselves to please them. They walked the Lebanese customers right through the door while the rest of us continued to wait in the queue. They ignored us the black customers".

This is appalling behaviour! Just because we are all black people, does not mean you should offer us poor service to ourselves. Black businesses are happy to sell expired food items to black people with the myth that expired food will not kill. Will they do that if their customers were non-black?

Black businesses should stop taking black customers for granted. All customers are the same no matter their ethnicity because WE ARE PAYING THE SAME PRICE FOR YOUR GOODS AND SERVICES.

Many of the respondents drew my attention to the fact that non-black businesses (especially Asian and Jewish businesses) are INWARD LOOKING because they look after their own. They lift each other up. On the other hand, black businesses are OUTWARD LOOKING because they treat other ethnic groups better than their fellow black customers.

There is a hierarchy in the level of service black customers receive from black businesses. This list shows who gets the best service with (1) being the best and (4) being the worst.

- Non-black customers first
- Followed by a wealthy customer or big tipper
- A new and unknown customer
- A known customer/family or friend.

#1 indicates that when these same black businesses with poor service standards serve non-black customers, they suddenly become more professional and respectful . Why is that?

A wealthy customer gets better service too, especially if they give big tips. An unknown black customer is next in line but they also get poor service. If black businesses treat customers they do not know badly, we can imagine how they would treat a family or friend who pays for a product or service. It is much worse and it is a pure case of FAMILIARITY BREEDING CONTEMPT. They expect you to accept crappy service because of the friend or family relationship.

I will not do this problem justice without discussing the apparent dislike that the Carribean black community have for their African counterparts. It is alleged that this is attributed to the fact that the Carribeans still blame the Africans for selling them into slavery centuries ago. I can empathise with this. However, it is important to state that our ancestors who committed that dastardly act are long dead and gone.

Their descendants are the ones living today . So the question is should the Carribeans continue to take this out on the innocent descendants who wholeheartedly condemn slavery and the act? Or should they put it behind them and move on by embracing their African 'brothers and sisters'. We may be different shades of black, but we are one race - the Black race.

HOW TO GET IT RIGHT

1. Treat all customers equally. Stop taking your black customers for granted. Treating non-black customers

better is a sign of an inferiority complex.

2. Every customer is important and valuable because they are paying the same price for your goods and services.
3. Do not expect your friends and family to accept poor or delayed service from you because they are paying for the service too, and they are usually the ones most likely to give you a referral or recommend you to someone else.
4. Do not chose who to serve on a queue. It is first come, first served.

NO REFUNDS

Africans are known to hold many superstitious beliefs. Therefore, I was not surprised when I learned about this one that is related.

It is a Yoruba adage from Western Nigeria.

> *"Tí á bá tí sé wó (gbá ówó) ní ââró Monday,*
> *kò sé dá pádà."*

(The English translation is - Once money has been collected from a customer, especially on a Monday, it is believed that refunding it will bring bad luck throughout that week hence no refund.)

This superstitious belief is widely held in black communities, especially by Africans - those back home in Africa and those in the diaspora. Black businesses are driven by a desire to make money as quickly as possible.

That is what drives the way they conduct business. How else do we explain the refusal to give a refund no matter what? I remember growing up in Nigeria with the realisation that if you buy something from the stores, you cannot take it back for a refund. I experienced that on numerous occasions. There was a joke that once money gets into the hand of a Nigerian trader, you will never get it back.

The best you can hope for is an exchange. To achieve that you should be prepared to go through an argument and even insults from the business owner before that exchange is made.

As we have read in the previous chapter, most of the respondents said they do not bother taking anything back for a refund because it is not worth the trouble you will get in the process.

In the United Kingdom, and in most Western countries, you have up to fourteen to thirty days to return an undamaged item for a full refund or exchange. Isn't that great?

Right to a refund

"(1) The right to a refund gives the consumer the right to receive a refund from the trader of all money paid by the

consumer for the digital content (subject to subsection).
(2) If the breach giving the consumer the right to a refund affects only some of the digital content supplied under the contract, the right to a refund does not extend to any part of the price attributable to digital content that is not affected by the breach.
(3) A refund must be given without undue delay, and in any event within 14 days beginning with the day on which the trader agrees that the consumer is entitled to a refund.
(4) The trader must give the refund using the same means of payment as the consumer used to pay for the digital content unless the consumer expressly agrees otherwise.
(5) The trader must not impose any fee on the consumer in respect of the refund."
www.legislation.gov.uk

Black businesses ignore this consumer rights and they get away with it, because we the Black customers allow them to do so.

HOW TO GET IT RIGHT

1. This is an obvious one. If the product or item is undamaged, give a refund or an exchange if that is what the customer wants. Remember the customer is always right.

2. Do not bring superstition into business because it has no place in it. Is there any proof that giving a refund on a Monday would ruin the rest of the week for your business? Think about this logically. If anything, giving a refund will encourage that customer to come back next time. What customer will want to patronise a business that cannot refund or exchange an item?
3. Familiarise or educate yourself on consumer rights. If you live in the West, you must have seen this practice when you have had to return an item yourself. Show your customers the same courtesy, otherwise you may not be able to get away with such unprofessional conduct much longer.

KNOWING WHEN TO DECLINE A NEW ORDER

The desire to make quick money drives everything black businesses do. This explains why they refuse to turn down a business order, even when they know they cannot meet the required deadline.

We have read about hairdressers and tailors who never say no to a new order. Caterers and cake makers are guilty of this too. They accept an order and leave the customer panicking when the delivery is delayed, or the deadline missed. How can you earn a customer's trust and repeat business if you do not do what you say you will do?

As a business owner, when I tell my black friends and family that I turned down an order they are always shocked. This is the reaction I get.

"Really?"

"Wow!"

"You actually turned it down?"

Why not? Sometimes it is the right thing to do to avoid disappointing the client. I prefer to put my business reputation first and foremost above money or profit. The thinking behind this is simple - it is my reputation of satisfying my customers' needs that will bring me referrals and that is the best for my business. If I accept the quick money and disappoint the customers, I would lose future income but will earn instant profit. Therefore, it is a no - brainer. I chose future income and a good reputation.

The inability to meet a customer's deadline is not the only problem that arises from never saying no to a customer. There are black businesses that do not have the skill or capability of delivering an order but take it on anyway. They accept the payment and leave the customer with unfinished and damaged items. In Chapter 2, we read Matthew's example; he paid a fellow Ugandan to design a website for him and it was never completed even after a year. He ended up paying someone else in the UK to do the job, thereby paying twice for the same work and waiting a year in the process.

In Chapter 4, we read about tailors who were still learning to make clothes but convinced their customers they could make dresses for them. The result was a disaster; damaged fabrics that could not be worn. Unsurprisingly, a refund was never given. Another example of unprofessional conduct.

NANA'S STORY

Nana saw the beautiful promotional bags created for a friend by a manufacturer based in Ghana. The promo bags were beautiful, and she needed to order some for her book launch.

The samples presented to her were fantastic designs. Therefore, Nana was happy to pay an upfront fee for the bags. When the bags arrived, it was a shoddy job. They did not look half as good as the samples that were presented to her.

There was no apology, and the business owner's attitude was quite bad. He blamed it on the urgency of the order, claiming if he had more time to deliver the order, the quality of the products would have been as good as the samples.

Nana was shocked to hear this because the business owner never informed her that he could not meet the deadline or that he required more time. Instead, he took the full payment upfront and did a shoddy job. This business owner should have turned down this order due to the tight deadlines. Unsurprisingly, Nana did not get a refund from the bag designer.

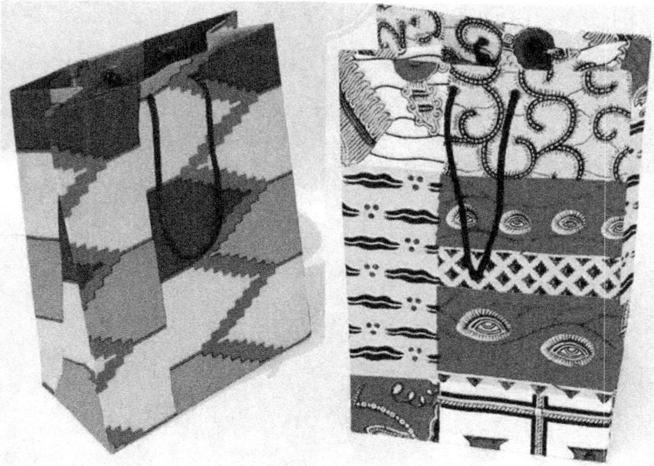

The beautiful bags presented to Nana.

The shoddy job delivered to Nana.

HOW TO GET IT RIGHT

1. Always manage expectations. If you are fully booked, let the customer know and offer them your next available date and give them a chance to decide if they want to proceed knowing that.
2. Treat your customers fairly and with respect.

Chapter Six

A Lesson In Pricing

> *"Quality is remembered long after the price is forgotten. The bitterness of poor quality is remembered long after the sweetness of low price has faded from memory."*
> ***- ALDO GUCCI***

Pricing of products and services by black businesses is another pain point that all the respondents asked me to highlight in this book. Some definitions are a good place to start.

"What Is Pricing?

"Pricing refers to the decision-making process that goes into establishing a value for a product or service. There are many different strategies that a business can use when setting prices, but they are all a form of pricing. The price that's set during the pricing process is what the customer will pay for that product or service."

THE THREE GENERAL APPROACHES TO PRICING

Cost-Based Pricing

"This approach ignores (in theory, but not always in practice) what other sellers are setting their prices for the same product or a similar one. Instead, this pricing strategy bases the selling price on its relation to cost."

Competitive Pricing

"Competitive pricing, as the name suggests, looks to the seller's competition before setting a price. Knowing the competition's prices can give you a framework for your pricing. You may decide to match the competition, undercut them, or, if you feel you offer a better product or service, charge more than them."

Demand-Based Pricing

"This approach responds primarily to movement in demand–whether it's waning or growing. If demand is growing, a seller may increase the selling price, especially as supply becomes more limited."

(Source: www.thebalancemoney.com)

One of the biggest issues that black businesses seem to struggle with is pricing. They tend to price themselves out of the market by charging a higher price than their competitors.

Research shows this can be attributed to not having enough capital to start the business in the first place. Or having to pay high interest rates on their business loans. Other reasons were lower traction and the high cost of wholesale prices from suppliers.

This explains why we find most black-owned African grocery stores cram their stores with anything they can sell. They sell hair products and even clothing items alongside the food products just to make enough profit to pay their suppliers and loan repayment. Even when the food item is going bad or about to expire, they refuse to reduce the price but will carry on trying to sell it. A good example is selling plantain.

PENNY WISE, POUND FOOLISH?

Plantain is a much-loved food item in the black community, especially for Africans. It is usually sold as two or three pieces for one pound sterling in the UK. When it is turning black and soft, which is a sign that it is rotting inside. You would expect the black businesses to reduce the price like their Asian/Arab competitors and sell it as buy one get one free or even four or five pieces for a pound.

Instead, they maintain the same price and unsurprisingly, black customers refuse to buy it. Therefore, they end up throwing the plantain in the bin. The same goes for yam and fruits. They could have cut the price for a day or two to sell off those food items, so they at least make some money instead of nothing at all. This is PENNY-WISE POUND-FOOLISH behaviour.

I have never seen a special offer at any African grocery stores for a BOGOF (buy one, get one free) or anything on sale. The Asian-owned African grocery stores always reduce the prices and sell those items off before they rot. Instead of two or three plantains for one pound, you get four or five plantain for a pound and customers love that. This is what a **demand-based pricing approach** looks like.

HIGHER / INAPPROPRIATE PRICING

The price is always one or two pounds higher than that of the Asian or Arab competition. As much as black customers want to patronise black businesses, we also want to spend less money on good quality products and great customer service. This is what we want, but hardly what we get. I do not think it is any surprise where we chose to shop. Black businesses should adopt the **competitive pricing approach** here.

The grocery stores are not the only ones who do this. Most Nigerian restaurants offer as little as five slices of fried plantain to go with the popular grilled fish meal which they sell to customers at a price between twenty to twenty-five pounds per meal. This is one that astounds many of my respondents because if you buy two or three pieces of plantain for a pound, then why can't the restaurants serve one whole fried plantain (about eight to ten slices)? There is no justification for why a twenty-five-pound meal does not deserve one plantain which costs only fifty pence.

Such businesses always end up losing their customers and it is no surprise why. Compare this to a Chinese restaurant whose meal prices could be as low as six to ten pounds. You can get a regular or large portion of fried rice with meat or chicken for less than ten pounds. Now we know why those businesses last for decades. Good food at affordable prices.

This is a good example of inappropriate pricing:

FLORENCE'S STORY

Florence (not her real name) paid an independent book publisher eight hundred pounds to publish a children's book with just twenty-six pages. Little did Florence know that the cost of publishing is largely based on the size of the book and the added cost of editing, formatting, book cover design and the various publishing versions like paperbacks, eBooks and audiobooks.

All these requirements would determine the cost of publishing the book because the smaller the book, the cheaper it is to publish and print. This is why I advocate that whatever service or product you are paying for, it is important that you at least know the basics about it. That would enable you to spot any RED FLAGS that you are being cheated.

Florence had no clue about book publishing. She did not sign a contract either, which would have indicated exactly what she was paying for. She paid over eight hundred pounds for the book publishing and her book was simply printed and multiple copies were handed over to her. She was scammed because the book was not set for global distribution on Amazon or other global distribution systems as is the norm for published books these days. Otherwise, how can you sell your book to the public without a distribution system? Florence was shocked and disappointed at this outcome.

A few months later, Florence found another independent publisher, a black business. They were happy to publish the book at less than half the amount she paid and also published an eBook version of the book as part of the deal. They explained to Florence that her book is quite small, so the standard price for book publishing will not apply because it will cost less to publish. This is what a fair pricing structure looks like. It is also an example of a **cost-based pricing approach**.

NO ADVANCE NOTICE ABOUT PRICE INCREASE

Price changes cannot be done overnight. Raising prices overnight without notifying customers in advance was also an issue raised by many of the respondents. There should be a warning in the form of a notice to customers that the prices would be raised and be effective on a stated date. It can be as simple as a notice on a piece of paper stuck to the wall in the business premises.

When I asked one food retailer why customers were not notified of the sudden fifty percent price increase, his response was this;

"Why should we? Just pick up the food item and I will tell you the price at the till".

There you have it. They do not understand that customers need to be notified in advance. Another food retailer told me that since everyone is suffering the pains of the rising cost of living in the country, they should not be surprised about the price increase.

SURPRISE EXTRA CHARGES

Transparency in pricing is very important. Whatever you want to charge a customer for has to be agreed beforehand to avoid disagreements and conflict. This is also about honest dealings. If the business has nothing to hide, they would run it by the customer first before incurring those expenses. The following true experience was shared by one of my respondents.

ARABA'S STORY

Araba (not her real name) had a builder in Ghana she has been contracting for years to work on her property, while she lived in England. Every quote he gave her was always a STARTING COST - an estimate.

When he gave Araba an invoice for the job done, there was always something they had to fix which she was never pre-notified about until it is alleged to have been fixed. Since she lived abroad, she could not verify the claims. The builder put other extra charges in the quote including some unknown transportation costs. She simply paid the invoice.

After this long business relationship, Araba trusted him. The builder took advantage of this trust and started to inflate the quotations he gave her by doubling the number of materials he needed for the building.

When she received a particularly high quote, she decided to seek a second opinion by getting a quote from another builder. To her greatest surprise, she received a quote that was half the price of the one from her regular builder. When she told her regular builder, he said,

"Let's see how that person can complete the job at that price".

The new builder completed the job and even had some building materials leftover. Araba fired her regular builder on the spot because she realised, he had been cheating her for a long time. She told all her friends and family about this terrible experience and none of them patronised that builder ever again.

HOW TO GET IT RIGHT

1. There is a lot of helpful information and examples above on the different approaches to pricing. I recommend that black businesses should consider using them going forward to improve their selling strategy.
2. Avoid giving out surprise extra charges. If you must charge more for a service, inform the customer before you do to get their buy-in.
3. Be fair with your pricing always. You cannot have the same prices for different products or services. Always consider the cost of producing that item so you can charge appropriately for it. Otherwise, the customer will find out they are being overcharged and you will lose that customer for good.

Chapter Seven

Untrained Business Staff

"Courteous treatment will make a customer a walking advertisement "
-James Cash Penney (Founder of JC Penney Stores)

This chapter should be about untrained employees that we usually find serving us at black business premises. However, I decided to address untrained business owners as well, because many of our black businesses are a 'one-man-show'. This means the business owner is the one who operates the business end-to-end. Therefore, the owner doubles as the staff.

You have read about many examples of poor-quality service standards and this can only be attributed to a lack of training. Maybe there was some form of business training or induction, but we do not know because we hardly see it reflected in the service we receive. This is what some respondents had to say about it:

"Their standards are quite low when it comes to customer service."
"Customer Service is non-existent".
"There is a complete lack of customer care".
"Substandard service and a nonchalant attitude to professionalism".

The human resource is arguably the most important asset a business has. All the respondents raised this issue of lack of training and business acumen exhibited by most black business owners. When we complain about poorly trained staff with very poor customer service skills, it is not a surprise because an untrained business owner does not have the necessary skills and expertise to train their staff.

Even our very educated black entrepreneurs and professionals with business acumen employ employees who do not know how to serve customers, and it is clear that they were either not trained or have a nonchalant attitude towards customer service and customer satisfaction.

Why are Employees regarded as a company's NUMBER ONE ASSET? Let's ponder this explanation.

"Why employees are important stakeholders. Your employees are the ones who create, manufacture, sell and deliver your products. They are crucial to your businesses' success or failure. They are invested in your company as you pay their wages and offer them job security."

(Source - www.myhrtoolkit.com)

- *Essential to providing goods or services.*
- *Employees are the face of an organisation.*

- *Employees are the base of a strong and long-running organisation.*
- *Employees are major contributors to the profits and worth of the organisation.*
- *Motivated employees make a significant difference.*

(Source - www.e-learningpartners.com)

- *Your people are your biggest resource and can affect public perception of your brand.*
- *Your employees are your brand ambassadors – the face of your company.*
- *Value your employees and staff, and you can increase your company's profitability.*

(Source - www.forbes.com)

We often see black employees on business premises look upset or angry as they show their problems on their faces. Why do they bring their personal problems to the workplace?

If they do not like you, they will treat you badly because they do not have the training to know you do not allow your personal feelings to cloud your judgement or influence your behaviour when you treat customers.

Non-black business owners and their staff make the effort to treat customers well and in a courteous manner no matter how they feel about you or whatever is going on in their lives. They are so good at this that you cannot tell that the person is racist or prejudiced.

All the respondents complained about long queues and extended waiting times due to poor service because the staff are busy on their phones instead of serving customers.

TRUE LIFE EXAMPLES

(A)

I once saw a waitress at an African restaurant sitting down with a male customer and flirting with him for an hour instead of serving customers. Customers complained about the long waiting times for their food orders and were completely ignored. The business owner fired the employee that same day as a deterrent to the others.

(B)

A respondent narrated her experience at a restaurant in Ghana, where the meals on the menu were priced to include seventy-five pesewas so they can get away with not giving you change of twenty-five pesewas. She came to this conclusion because every time she ate at this restaurant, the waiters always informed her that they did not have coins for the twenty-five pesewas change. This was what they subjected customers to and since they do not accept card payments, they could get away with it because it was such a little amount of money. The respondent tried to beat them at their game and insisted on waiting for her change. The waiters turned rude and grumpy after that, but they had no choice but to give it to her. However, they made sure it took a long time by making her wait a while for the change in the hope that it would discourage her from waiting for it. Instead, she waited patiently.

When I heard this narrative, my initial thought was that the business owner must be in on it. He must have set those prices deliberately. On second thought, it could be the staff trying to keep the change for themselves. In any case, this is the wrong thing to do.

RECRUITMENT PRACTICES

A key reason attributed to the lack of training is many because black business owners see training as a waste of money and so do not train their staff.

Small and medium sized black businesses fail to pay the right wages as well because they see it subliminally that they are doing you a favour. For example, they hire people as a favour to a friend or relative, thereby taking on people who are poorly skilled, and they don't provide the training for them.

In Africa, there are no employment rights and basic employee benefits except you work for large corporations. It is hire and fire. No efficient system in place for reference checks. People usually get jobs via word-of-mouth and personal relationships in our business community. For example, the HR landscape in Nigeria does not allow for robust practices. There is little training, and limited health benefits.

At least in Nigeria and other parts of Africa, they employ staff in the business. What you find with small and medium sized black businesses in the west is that they often refuse to hire staff even when the business desperately requires one. Many put it down to inability to find someone trustworthy. It is more likely because they are unwilling to employ the right person and pay them the right wage.

They fail to recruit, to the detriment of the business. Even those that have employees notice a remarkably high turnover of staff because they often stay for a short period and resign soon after which is attributed to the very low wage. Many recruit illegal immigrants who are undocumented and pay them below the minimum wage.

STELLA'S STORY

A black woman opened the only African grocery shop in a city in England. Let's name her Stella for the purpose of this narrative. Stella did not employ anyone to help out with the long hours needed to operate a grocery store. She opened the store at 9:30 am because she had to drop her kids off at school. Stella closed the store between 3 and 4:30 pm to go do the school run. She returned to the store but had to close for the day at 7 pm, when customers returning from work usually do their grocery shopping.

Stella was always stressed because she was juggling running the business and her parental responsibilities. She wore her problems on her face; she was always miserable looking and treated customers rudely and with an unwelcoming attitude. Her irregular opening hours and bad attitude soon put customers off and many stopped patronising the store. Stella had the belief that black African customers had no choice but to patronise her because she was the only African grocery store in the town. That is a misconception many black grocers have. They forget the big stores like Tesco and Sainsbury that have branches located all over the country have a section in their stores entirely dedicated to selling foods for black and Asian customers named WORLD FOODS. These big stores were not the only competition Stella had to deal with.

An Asian owned African grocery store opened opposite Stella's store and stole all her customers. They opened at 6am and closed at 9pm. As I mentioned in chapter six, their prices are usually lower and service standards are higher. They tick all the boxes, so it is a no brainier that they would attract the black African customers.

Stella's store did not last long after that, and within 12 months of setting up the business, Stella had to shut it down. Not even the inclusion of selling hair products and clothing in her store made the required difference. If only she had employed a cashier or customer service staff, to take the burden off her and keep the store open throughout business hours.

- Was she unable to afford hiring a staff?
- Did she have money trouble? Was she paying back a small business loan for setting up the business?
- Or was she just trying to reduce her cost of running the business and maximise her profits?

I interviewed a few black businesses about this issue and the responses will be found in part 3 of this book.

HOW TO GET IT RIGHT

1. Hire a part-timer if you cannot afford a full-time staff.
2. If you were in paid employment, would you leave the office whenever you wanted to go do the school run? The answer is no! You either arrange for childcare or work part-time. So, the question is this - Is your business a part-time business or a full-time business? These are important things to consider before starting the business in the first place because you cannot make it up as you go along. Managing or operating a successful business is a huge commitment.

3. Forget about your problems and woes as soon as a customer walks into your business premises and give them a charming smile. Welcome them because that is how you get customers to spend even more than they intended when they walked into your store. Engage them in brief chit-chat about their day and family. Black people love that. Do this because it is also the professional thing to do. Always ask yourself this question - *'will I do this in paid employment?'*
4. If you are a black business, and you hire people, please train them. The training does not have to be expensive anymore. There are so many FREE video tutorials these days that are available online, especially on YouTube. Take advantage of this and get your staff to watch them and quiz them about it. As the business owner you require training too, because if you do not value professionalism and high service standards you will not be able to implement them in your business.
5. If you have the only African or Carribean grocery store in a town, that is not a reason to take your black customers for granted. Even if you sell the best products or have great demand for your products or service, do not become complacent. That monopoly you are enjoying never lasts long. Competition usually appears after a while. Continue to show your customers that they are important and valuable to you so you can gain their

trust and loyalty. That way the competition cannot steal them from you. Remember customers always have a choice of who to buy from; some are happy to travel a longer distance to buy a product if they do not want to patronise your business.

Chapter Eight

Unethical Practices

There are a lot of unethical practices exhibited by many of our black business owners all over the world. It is worse in some parts of the world than others, and research has shown that it is down to the value system of the individuals as well as the communal value system. Let's look at some definitions.

> *"Values can be defined as broad preferences concerning appropriate courses of actions or outcomes. As such, values reflect a person's sense of right and wrong or what "ought" to be. Values tend to influence attitudes and behaviour and these types include ethical/moral values".*
> *"A value system is a set of consistent values used for the purpose of ethical or ideological integrity. As a member of a society, group or community, an individual can hold both a personal value system and a communal value system at the same time."*
> *(Source: www.wikipedia.org)*

Our value system determines what we consider right or wrong. It also shows what we reward and what we punish. So, what is our value system as black people? Let's check out the key values that are applicable to this topic:

WHAT WE REWARD AND VALUE

- University education
- Making money
- Being more successful than others

WHAT WE DO NOT PUNISH

- Running a cash-based business
- Sexual harassment in the workplace and business.
- Corruption and fraud

There are many unethical practices raised by the respondents, which includes black solicitors who have lost their licences due to malpractices - such as embezzling conveyancing funds meant for mortgage transactions and are now unable to practice in the UK.

The list is quite extensive, but I will only focus on the two key unethical practices, which were highlighted by most of the respondents. They are:

FRAUDULENT PRACTICES.

Receiving full payment for a job but not delivering the order or taking money from customers under false pretences, especially when they cannot or do not know how to do that work.

The reason why some black businesses find it easy to defraud customers, especially in Africa is because there is no accountability and consequences to serve as a deterrent to others. We do not PUNISH it as we should.

In addition, businesses that do such things tend to aim it at fellow black people because they know they can get away with it if it is a black customer. They deliver bad products or services and we do not inform the police. Unsurprisingly, the police in Africa are corrupt as well, so are quite unreliable.

When black businesses deal with non-black customers in the West, they are more professional and cautious in their dealings because there are laws and law enforcement agencies to protect the customers.

As I mentioned in chapters four and five of this book, some Black businesses sell us expired products and we do nothing about it. They refuse to give us a refund and we do nothing about it. There is no accountability and no punishment, so that is why black people use the phrase "ANYTHING GOES" to describe the nonchalant attitude to consumer rights and regulations in most African countries and countries in the Caribbean.

NOT DOING THINGS BY THE BOOK

"There are many thousands of black-owned firms in Africa, but few of them are formal, registered firms and even fewer are medium-size or large businesses".
(Source - www.cgdev.org)

Many black businesses are not registered for trading and many of them only accept cash payments. It is unbelievable that this still happens today despite the COVID pandemic this new world where cash payments are often rejected because they could contain the COVID virus.

I have a suspicion that many black businesses may be ignorant of the benefits of registering a business, paying VAT, or having a payroll system in place. Therefore, I am going to share very important information here about the benefits of doing business by the book, using the UK as an example.

I interviewed a brilliant black accountant in the UK, who gave me an insight into this issue. Before you start a business, the first main consideration is the business legal entity. What does this mean?

> *"A* ***business entity*** *is an entity that is formed and administered as per corporate law in order to engage in business activities, charitable work, or other activities allowable. Most often, business entities are formed to sell a product or a service. There are many types of business entities defined in the legal systems of various countries. These include corporations, cooperatives, partnerships, sole traders, limited liability companies and other specifically permitted and labelled types of entities. The specific rules vary by country and by state or province. Some of these types are listed below, by country."*

For guidance, approximate equivalents in the company law of English-speaking countries are given in most cases, for example:

- *private company limited by shares or Ltd. (United Kingdom, Ireland, and the Commonwealth)*
- *public limited company (United Kingdom, Ireland, and the Commonwealth)*
- *limited partnership*
- *general partnership*
- *chartered company*
- *statutory corporation*
- *state-owned enterprise*
- *holding company*
- *subsidiary company*
- *sole proprietorship*
- *charitable incorporated organisation (UK)*
- *reciprocal inter-insurance exchange*

However, the regulations governing particular types of entities, even those described as roughly equivalent, differ from jurisdiction to jurisdiction. When creating or restructuring a business, the legal responsibilities will depend on the type of business entity chosen."

(Source - www.wikipedia.org)

Some black businesses trade for a year or two before registering their business. Why do they do that?

Is it due to tax avoidance? Or a lack of knowledge about business legal entities?

UK TAX THRESHOLD

It was interesting to learn that companies do not pay tax until they make a profit. Only the profit is taxed. A business can also get tax relief. If you have two companies and one of them is making a loss and the other is making a profit, the profitable company will absorb the loss of the other company. To take advantage of this loss relief, you have to register a holding company, so you can have both companies as subsidiaries of the holding company. This is all legal.

VAT - VALUE ADDED TAX

"Value Added Tax (VAT) is levied on the majority of products and services offered by VAT-registered firms in the United Kingdom. It also applies to some EU and non-EU products and services imported into the UK. Businesses that are VAT-registered add VAT to the price of goods and services they offer to both commercial and non-commercial customers".

(Source - www.lidertax.co.uk)

VOLUNTARY VAT REGISTRATION

- You can choose to register for VAT if your turnover is less than £85,000 a year.
- You must pay HM Revenue and Customs (HMRC) any VAT you owe from the date they register you.
- If everything you sell is exempt from VAT, you do not have to register for VAT.

COMPULSORY REGISTRATION

You must register if, by the end of any month, your total VAT taxable turnover for the last 12 months was over £85,000.
You have to register within 30 days of the end of the month when you went over the threshold. Your effective date of registration is the first day of the second month after you go over the threshold.
(Source - www.gov.uk)

VAT EXEMPTION

"If a supply is exempt from VAT, it may be because the EU considers the goods or services as essential. VAT exempt supplies include:

- *Education and training*

- *Insurance, finance and credit Fundraising events by charities.*
- *Medical treatments provided by hospitals.*
- *Subscriptions to membership organisations*
- *Selling, leasing and letting of commercial land and buildings – though authorities can waive this exemption".*

(Source - www.sovos.com)

What are the benefits of being VAT registered?

- *You'll appear to be a bigger business if you're charging VAT, as the current limit for compulsory registration is £85,000 on VATable turnover (2023/24).*
- *If you sell to VAT registered businesses they can reclaim the VAT from HMRC so your selling price is still competitive and you will be able to recover the VAT on your costs.*
- *Maintaining up to date records will provide better information for running your business.*
- *You can claim VAT on certain items that you purchased prior to the date of VAT registration. Talk to your accountant about the exact details.*
- *If you are in a VAT reclaim situation, then you will definitely be better off.*

- *You're likely to receive repayments because your VATable sales are lower than your VATable costs. This may be because you're accumulating stock or because your sales are below the standard rate of 20% at either the reduced rate of 5% or zero rate 0%."*

(*Source* - www.starlingbank.com)

PAYROLL REGISTRATION

Many black businesses do not register for payroll. It is very important to register for payroll to ensure your National Insurance (NI) is credited even if you earn below the threshold of £125 per week (about £500 a month). This way everyone who pays NI gets a state pension.

To qualify for state pension in the UK, you must have worked for a minimum of eleven years and a maximum of forty-four years.

Class I National Insurance - employed.

Class 2 National Insurance - Self-employed

If a business owner does not register for payroll for themselves and their employees, they could be depriving everyone affected the all-important state pension in their old age or when they retire.

SEXUAL HARASSMENT IN THE WORKPLACE

Sexual harassment in the workplace is very rampant in our community. Anyone who studied at a university in Africa knows about this. Lecturers openly threaten female students that they would not pass a module or even graduate from the university unless they have sex with them. As a woman who studied at a university in Africa in the 90s, I can confirm that such threats and sexual harassment were commonplace.

I was lucky it never happened to me in university and that was because I had an uncle in the university who was also a lecturer, so the other lecturers had to leave me alone.

Many respondents confirmed that it is still happening today in 2023. Sexual harassment in African universities is now done with impunity. It is no longer done secretly like it was done decades ago. It is simply worse now because there are no consequences.

These were young girls who are completely helpless. Men in positions of power take advantage of their female students who are often young enough to be their daughters. The university authorities do not interfere in such matters, as such they were never addressed. Parents are helpless too, unless you are from a wealthy or influential family, preferably a politician. Then the lecturers would leave you alone.

Women do not bother reporting such matters to the police or the press because it has become normalised. Sad isn't it? As though trying to study for a degree wasn't tough enough, you had to contend with sexual harassment as well.

Even in Hollywood, movie directors and music producers use their power to sexually harass women, so it was a universal problem until the 'Me Too' movement helped to put a stop to it. Why hasn't it stopped in the black business community? Unfortunately, the 'Me Too' movement has not done much for the black community in Africa.

NORMALISING THE ABNORMAL

From university and other higher education to the workplace, senior colleagues in most organisations threaten junior colleagues that they will lose their jobs if they do not have sex with them. Men are not the only ones harassing their junior female colleagues, women do it to junior male colleagues too. The women who date their bosses get favours such as career advancement, getting promoted into jobs they may not be qualified for.

In some Nigerian banks, customers ask female bankers for sexual favours in return for opening million Naira accounts or fixed deposit accounts with the bank.

The bank executives turn a blind eye to their employees suffering sexual harassment at the hands of customers. This is common knowledge and it baffles me that this is allowed to happen at workplaces in Africa. This all boils down to our value system. We should punish sexual harassment of women but our society does not. What you reward and what you punish is directly linked to what you value. Sexual harassment and stealing has become normalised in our society and community.

With academic institutions and big corporations engaging in such unethical practices, it is no surprise that other medium to small business owners are also doing the same. When you try to conduct business with some black business owner, do not be surprised if he/she makes a pass at you before they proceed with the business deal. Age doesn't matter; some are so unprofessional and perverted that they refuse to do business with you unless you date them. You are trying to patronise that business, but they give you this condition as though you are doing them a favour. It beggars belief.

This is one example a respondent shared with me. Let's call her Theodora. She wanted to order personalised boxes from a black business owner. After assuring her he could deliver the items, she waited to receive a quote for the order. She never received it. She sent text messages to chase it up and this was the conversation that ensued. (Charles is not his real name.)

Charles: Grand rising, young lady.

Theodora: Grand rising, Charles. How are you today?

Charles: Hi young lady, are you going to tuck me in bed and read me a story?

Theodora: Are you flirting with me, Charles?

Charles: My darling. My intent is to love you. But love and execution in the business arena is the norm.

Theodora: I cannot promise the love bit, but I am happy to do business with you. I hope we can work together without the love part in the way.

Theodora did not hear from him for weeks. When she contacted him again, this was the outcome.

Theodora: Hey Charles! Still waiting for an update on the quote for those boxes.

Charles: So sorry I forgot. Regards, Charles.

That was it. Theodora never heard from him again.

People behave this way with others they presume to share their value system or at least have an understanding of it. That is why such behaviour is from a black person to another black person.

I must add that the prevalence of such unethical behaviour depends on where you live in the world as a black person. If you live in Africa and the Carribeans, then this would be commonplace. In the West, sexual harassment is not acceptable behaviour and will be frowned upon and punished.

HOW TO GET IT RIGHT

1. If you fancy a customer, it is better to finish the business transaction before asking them out on a date or telling

them how you feel. Taking advantage of the situation and giving them conditions to do business with you is so unprofessional and unethical that it is unbelievable that many black businesses are still doing it. It is clearly a conflict of interest, and it is not rocket science to figure this out.

2. When one person tries to enforce consequences, someone will be brought in to beg you not to enforce it. Some even involve their church leader or pastor to intervene and the matter will be forgotten. Please enforce consequences if you can. Do not let anyone talk you out of it otherwise, our society will never stop these unethical practices.

Chapter Nine

Are Black Businesses Too Lazy To Make Money?

"If you are not taking care of your customers, your competitor will".

- Bob Hooey

This is a controversial topic because you may be wondering how black can people be too lazy to make money when we have clearly established that as a community, we like to make money.

The answer is simple; many black businesses like to make money very quickly and in the easiest way possible. We like to be paid upfront for everything and one hundred percent of the amount if possible. Once that payment is received in full, many black businesses tend not to care about the execution or completing the job. That is the 'hit-and-run' business mindset and the preceding chapters are full of examples of that. In chapter four, Tessy hired a builder who did the job for two days, got paid and abandoned the project.

Black businesses are sometimes too lazy to draw up a contract or do any paperwork for conducting a business. Everything is done by word of mouth and informally. There are so many examples to share in this chapter, but I will focus on the main ones raised by the respondents.

BUSINESS OPENING HOURS

Most black businesses are known for late opening times and early closing times compared to their non-black counterparts.

Black businesses

- Monday - Friday - Opens at 11 am and closes at 6 pm.
- Saturday (busiest days for business) - they close at 6 pm to go clubbing and partying (especially Carribeans and African Americans do this).
- Sunday's - open even later at noon or 1 pm because they were partying the night before.

I must point out that there is nothing wrong with having a good time and letting your hair down if it is done occasionally. Clubbing every weekend to the extent that it impacts the success of your business is a big problem. Closing the business premises early to go home is a sign that you are not serious about your business. You have to put the hard work and the hours in if you want customers to take you seriously. A respondent in the Southeast of London complained about an African takeaway franchise in his neighbourhood that opens at 12 pm and closes at 6 pm. This is absurd because 6 pm is dinnertime and arguably the busiest time of the day for a takeaway or any food business.

Some takeaway franchise restaurants like McDonald's are open for twenty-four hours, or from 5 am - 2 am. The latest opening times are 7 am and the earliest closing times are midnight. As black customers we do not expect all black takeaway businesses to be open for 24 hours or from 5 am - 2 am, however opening times from 12 pm - 6 pm is simply outrageous. I think our restaurants and stores can do better than that.

ASIAN AND ARAB BUSINESSES

- Mondays - Fridays - open at 6 am and close at 10 pm. Then they stay back to do stock taking and plan how to make even more sales the next day.
- Saturdays - same thing because it is their busiest day.
- Sundays - opens 8 or 9 am

Black businesses open four or five hours after their Asian and other non-black counterparts. By the time the black business opens, their competitors have made plenty of sales and they will still be open long after the black businesses have closed. Smart black business owners have resorted to employing Asians and Arabs in their stores because they are more hardworking.

This probably explains why there are not many Off licence stores owned or managed by a black business owner, because they would have to stay open late into the night. Most Off licence stores in the UK are owned by Asians and Arabs. That says it all to me.

In Africa, many black businesses do not open on Sundays, and it may be mainly due to religious obligations, just the same way Jews do not open their shops on Saturdays. Muslims do not close their stores on Fridays though. They simply, shut it briefly to go to the mosque and they reopen the store later to continue trading.

Is it that most black businesses do not like hard labour if they can help it? Is perseverance not our strong suit? Once money is not being made, we tend to give up and move on to something else.

FRANCES AND CHRISSY'S STORY

Frances and Chrissy wanted to have a meeting at a black-owned African restaurant in London. They called to enquire about the opening times, and they were informed that it is 1 pm on a Saturday. They were happy with that and booked a table for their appointment.

Saturday arrived and both ladies turned up in front of the restaurant at exactly 12:59 pm. They knew that because they checked their arrival time. To their astonishment, the restaurant was not open. They could not believe it. Chrissy called the owner of the restaurant who was an acquaintance of hers. He did not answer the call, so she left a voicemail that they were standing in front of the restaurant waiting to go in and it was closed.

After five minutes of waiting outside the restaurant, Frances and Chrissy decided they needed another venue to have their meeting. They found a nice Italian restaurant a few blocks down the road. When they walked in, they found the restaurant full of customers and they were greeted by a very friendly waiter who took their order and served them a very delicious meal. They had a lovely time at that restaurant.

While they were having their meal, the owner of the restaurant called to blame Chrissy for turning up too early and that they did not expect her to be so punctual. He then gave the excuse that the waitress who was responsible for opening the restaurant overslept, and turned up late. He asked Chrissy and Frances to come back to the now-opened African restaurant. Chrissy refused and told him that they found an alternative restaurant and they liked it there. Such tales of disappointment happen all the time because I received many like this from the respondents.

Why was the Italian restaurant open from 9 am and busy serving many customers at 1 pm when their African counterparts could not be bothered to open at 1 pm? This buttresses the point that we are definitely too lazy to make money.

TOO LAZY TO MAKE IMPROVEMENTS / OR BE INNOVATIVE

Black businesses tend to be too lazy to make improvements to their products or services. They keep selling or doing the same thing year after year without trying to do things better to the satisfaction of their customers.

- Why the same menu with just Jollof rice when there is demand for fried rice?
- Why sell Suya and Moin-moin only on Fridays and Saturdays, when it is in high demand seven days a week?
- Why do only birthday cakes despite many requests for wedding cakes)?
- Why are African auntie hairdressers only doing braids and crotchet when there is demand for false lashes and wig fittings?
- Why only publish eBooks and paperbacks despite high demand for hardbacks and audiobooks.

What is stopping you from offering Suya and moin-moin and fried rice every day? Why are you too lazy to do wedding cakes or publish hardbacks and audiobooks for your clients? It is a win-win because you increase your sales and customer base.

HOW TO GET IT RIGHT

1. Be competitive - try to match the opening times of other businesses in that industry. Consider your customers when you decide on opening times.
2. If there is a skill gap because you lack the necessary skills to improve your product and service offerings, then you should learn that skill.
3. We need our black businesses to succeed beyond the first year or two.

Chapter Ten

Longevity In Business

"If you want to build a business that lasts, banks, breweries, and postal services are a good bet".
- Frank Jacobs

All the respondents raised the problem of a lack of longevity in black businesses. They emphasised the fact that many black businesses tend to shut down within a year or two. Why?

I argued about this initially, until I was asked to name any generational black-owned business that I knew in my home country, Nigeria. To my utter surprise, I could not name one. We researched it and we could not find many black businesses that have been passed on from one generation to the next. Most of the oldest black-owned companies have been bought over by new owners instead of remaining in the family. I decided to research the oldest black business worldwide. These were my findings:

OLDEST BLACK BUSINESSES IN THE USA

- *"E.E. Ward Moving and Storage is the oldest black business in the USA. (founded in 1881 by* ***John T. Ward****, an Underground Railroad conductor with his son, William, in Columbus, Ohio. Now it's a multimillion-dollar, award-winning company).*

- *NC Mutual - Life insurance company. One of the oldest black-owned life insurance companies in the country. (Founded in 1898 by an entrepreneur barber, John C Merrick who saturated the company because black people were ignored by other insurance companies).*
- *The Philadelphia Tribune (Founded in 1884 by Christopher J Perry at age 28. "Started as voice for the Black community during a time when they struggled to be heard or even recognized. Today, The Philadelphia Tribune has wracked up several awards for its stellar journalism and even publishes other newspapers."*
- *W.H. Jefferson Funeral Home. (Founded in 1894 by* ***William H.*** *and* ***Lucy C. Jefferson)*** *"Not only is this the oldest Black-owned funeral home in Mississippi, but it may be the oldest in the country. It is also one of the first funeral homes to have two burial insurance companies."*
- ***McKissack & McKissack*** *(Founded in 1905)* ***Moses McKissack III*** *and his brother,* ***Calvin L. McKissack****, start their own architecture firm in Nashville, Tennessee. Becoming one of the first Black American licensed architects in the country. Today, the company continues to land contracts on renovating and constructing new buildings and add-ons for airports, universities, major cities, museums, hospitals and more."*

(Source - www.michiganchronicle.com)

These five companies have been around for over a century and that is applaudable. It is good to see that the black community in America did not allow the slavery of their forefathers and ancestors to deter them from achieving such great feats. Some family-owned companies that have been around for over a hundred years usually have to change ownership for various reasons that is often beyond their control. As a black person I was glad to see many black owned businesses that have been around for centuries.

When I extended my research to the oldest BLACK-OWNED businesses in Africa and Afro Caribbeans, it was a different story. There was very little information available about this. Instead, I learnt that the oldest businesses in Africa were not founded by black people. Instead, they were founded by the white Europeans who colonised Africa and the Carribeans. This is not entirely surprising given the history of these two regions. It was sad to see that none of these oldest companies were founded by black people in our own continent of black people.

CARIBBEANS

- *Mount Gay Rum - (Barbados 1703)*
- *Rose Hall - (Jamaica 1770)*
- *House of Angostura - (Trinidad & Tobago 1830)*
- *Banks Dih - (Guyana 1840)*
- *Rhum Barbancourt - (Haiti 1862)*

(Source: www.reddit.com*)*

AFRICA

- *Groot Constantine – (South Africa 1685)*
- *Mauritius Post – (Mauritius 1772)*
- *Old Mutual Limited – (South Africa 1845)*
- *Bakers Limited – (South Africa 1851)*
- *First Bank of Nigeria – (Nigeria 1894).*

(Source - *www.smepeaks.com)*

The reason why these businesses survived for centuries was attributed to this:

> *"The above-mentioned oldest companies in Africa have experienced the worst business scenario one can ever imagine yet remain in business till date. Trust among staff in an organisation, willingness to take a*

risk when needed, a positive outlook, customer-centric approach and perseverance are factors that enabled them to prevail. "

(Source - www.smepeaks.com)

I was relieved to find that the ownership of some of these centuries-old businesses has transferred to indigenous black owners and management teams and are still successful today.

What stood out to me was the word PERSEVERANCE as one of the factors responsible for their success and longevity. It is the most important factor because even if you have a positive outlook and are customer-centric, your business will not survive unless you are willing to persevere through the difficult times that every business has to experience as a rite of passage. I think that is the main reason most new black businesses don't last beyond the first twelve months today.

Many of the respondents concluded that we seem to give up too quickly when the business starts to struggle. We want our profit right away, which is why we are quick to shut down the business once it becomes unprofitable. Perseverance is not our strong suit. Many black businesses set up a business just to make money instead of focusing on establishing the business first so that profit follows. Even when the money comes quickly, they go splashing it on cars and partying, instead of investing it back into the business.

Some respondents stated that this is also the reason why many black business partnerships fail. One party wants to spend the profit while the other wants to reinvest it in the business. We shall analyse the issue of black business partnerships later in this book.

Sometimes, black businesses do not last long because they are often one-man businesses, with the sole owner bearing all the risks. As an example, we met the African grocer, Stella in chapter seven. Like most black business owners, Stella carried a hundred percent risk and also had fewer ideas on how to make the business successful. All she could think of was to extend her products range from groceries to Afro hair products and African clothing. These made little difference due to the other problems she had to deal with, which I highlighted. Stella eventually lost out to her nearby competitors.

We are good at starting a business, but not running it. This is because we start wrong and then we run into trouble. We do not do a thorough market research and business plan by doing a SWOT analysis to understand the important factors of our business environment:

- S - STRENGTHS
- W - WEAKNESSES
- O - OPPORTUNITIES
- T - THREATS

This lack of market research, SWOT analysis and a business plan explains why most black businesses do not succeed beyond the first twelve months. We want black businesses to succeed beyond the first year or two to become generational businesses.

Black businesses rarely pass on from generation to generation. Why is that? Most times, the founder of the business outlives the business. Why do most black businesses shut down or are sold off once the founder passes away? Is it because we do not plan for the next generation?

Black businesses owners of large corporations or conglomerates are wealthy and usually send their children to the best schools in the world. As we Africans know, parents push their children to study for degrees preferably to become a doctor or a lawyer instead of involving them in the business early on like the non-black owned business owners do.

After graduating with a degree in a profession that they are passionate about and more interested in, taking over the family business is no longer a consideration or what they desire.

I have seen many situations where black parents force their children to take over the family business at an older age. They reluctantly accept the responsibility and take ownership. However, as soon as the parent, (business owner) dies, the children sell the business to a new owner.

Asians and Jews have more success with generational business because they start early on by getting their children involved in the business as teenagers. Even if they are engaged in university education, they buy into the idea of running the family business one day and they actually look forward to it. This strategy has been proven to work.

I have noticed that when the business is a law firm or a private hospital, accounting firm, or pharmacy and the children went to university to study that specific profession which is the family business, it becomes easier to pass on the business from one generation to the next. That being said, we could not name any of such professional generational businesses. If you know any that would be good. I bet there are some of them in the USA at least.

Some respondents also blamed this problem on our value system. I cannot help but agree with them. Our value system prioritises a university education over any other form of education. In the black community, especially in Africa, we value a university education as a high priority because it is seen as a route to a good job and a better life. This explains the joke that most Nigerians you meet have master's degrees and that has become the minimum qualification for Nigerians. A Bachelor's degree is not special anymore because almost everyone has it these days.

For a continent plagued by intense poverty, who can blame them? That explains why black owners of big corporations send their children to university for a degree qualification instead of allowing them to start working in the company early on to learn the ropes and grow through the ranks.

So, how about tradespersons and artisans in the black community? Are those not important vocations, too?

Unfortunately, tradespersons and artisans are not well paid or valued in Africa. The importance of the services provided by this category of workers in our community cannot be overemphasised, because no society can function without them. In the West, tradespersons are valued and some earn more income than university graduates. That being said, a Black African tradesperson is not easy to find in the West, but you will find Artisans. This is due to our value system.

WHO IS A TRADESPERSON AND ARTISAN?

> *"A **tradesperson** is a skilled worker that specializes in a particular trade. Tradespeople usually gain their skills through work experience, on-the-job training, an apprenticeship program or formal education."*

A Welder

(Source – www. en.m.wikipedia.org)

These are jobs or professions that "rely heavily on physical exertion". Tradespersons are welders, auto mechanics, electricians, builders, labourers, cleaning labourers, bus drivers, train and truck drivers, gardeners, Hairdressers, etc.

"An Artisan is a skilled craftsperson who builds, creates or makes objects either completely or partly by hand"

- *Jewellery making*
- *Clothing design*
- *Furniture making (also called cabinet making)*
- *Homeware design (such as Knifemaking)*

- *Watchmaking / Clockmaking*
- *Food production*
- *Beer brewing*
- *Wine production*
- *Sign writing*

PART TWO

The Overriding Schools of Thought about Black Businesses

(Source - www.whoosreading.com)

Chapter Eleven

The Myth That Black People Cannot Collaborate

'Together We Stand, Divided We Fall'
- Aesop, Ancient Greek storyteller.

There is a myth that black people cannot collaborate because we find it difficult to work together on anything for a long period. It usually falls apart or collapses after a while, whether it is doing business or simply working together to achieve the same goal. Envy and a desire to outdo each other quickly rears its ugly head and tears that collaborative group apart.

POSSIBLE ORIGINS

One of the respondents stated that our black community is 'programmed to think COMPETITION while most non-black communities think COLLABORATION. He attributed the origin of this problem to the 'divide and conquer rule' that some European governments used to colonise Africa and other black communities. Is this true? Ponder this: What is divide and conquer?

"It refers to a strategy for maintaining power that involves getting the people reporting to you to fight among themselves so they can't band together to overthrow you. In other words, "divide and rule" is the

strategy of keeping one's subordinates or opponents under control by fostering disagreement among them to stop them from banding together in opposition."
(Source: www.theidioms.com)

This could be true and may be partly to blame for why we cannot collaborate as black people. However, when we consider the fact that other non-black communities like the Asians were also colonised by the British with the same divide and conquer rule, why have they not turned out competitive like us? How have they been able to collaborate so well, and we do not?

Right there in our black community, there are some tribes or groups of people who understand collaboration and are able to do it very well. A well-known one to most Nigerians are the Igbo tribe. This is a case of nature versus nurture. The Igbos are nurtured to be enterprising and collaborative. They are very good at creating business clusters. They take on an apprentice and within a few years, they collaborate within the community to raise funds and set up a store for that apprentice, which he eventually owns and pays back the loan to set up that business.

Another 'tribe' of black people who know how to collaborate are the Somalians. They pulled money together to set up internet cafes and mobile phone accessories stores all over the UK when it was the trend. This is similar to what the

Asians do. It shows that in the same country of black people, you can have people who behave entirely differently from other tribes in that country. Therefore, I came to the logical conclusion that it is not in our nature to be competitive. We could be nurtured to have a collaborative mindset.

WHY ARE WE COMPETITIVE?

First and foremost, I want to explore why black people are competitive. To non-black communities, success means lifting others up or making others successful too.

Success to a black person means they are more successful than the other black people around them or in their immediate circle of friends and family. It means driving a bigger and better car than anyone else and living in a bigger house than anyone else even if you have a small family. Do we need those huge properties or large cars? No, we do not, but it is about keeping up appearances.

I admire the white people who drive small cars and live in small houses or flats in the UK. They understand that the bigger your car, the higher your insurance and road tax, so their motivation is to reduce their expenses as much as possible. They also downsize their properties once they retire, and their children have moved out. Construction companies build retirement estates for such people, and they are only one or two-bedroom flats. The concept of downsizing your property in the black community is seen as proof of financial difficulty instead of financial brilliance.

SIGNS OF COMPETITIVE BEHAVIOUR

They usually refuse to share any helpful tips to enable a fellow black person to succeed in that same career or business. This is probably why many black businesses copy without the know-how. A black business owner wants to be 'the one-eyed man in the village of blind people'; doing better than others in any way is their sign of success. One respondent recounted situations where new businesses on the same block try to bring down a fellow black business. It is apparently quite common with black entrepreneurs because they like to outdo each other.

You will know you are competitive if you refuse to give out such helpful information when a fellow black person asks you for it. These are some common examples:

- "What a beautiful dress! Where did you buy it?"
- "I am looking for a drama /swimming/ballet class for my daughter? Which one does your daughter attend?"
- "Where did you do your project management training? Can you refer me please or just give me the name (not even a fifty pounds incentive would sway a competitive person)"

- "What certifications do I need to do for a scrum master job? Which ones did you do?"
- "How do I start a coaching business like yours? I have the expertise as well as the skills and knowledge, so I could be good at it"
- "Wow! your hair looks so beautiful. Who is your stylist? Can you refer me?"
- "Are they recruiting in your place of work? Any suitable roles? I need a job badly".

The list is endless.

If you gladly share the information asked above, then you are not a competitive person. If you are reluctant to share such information, then you should ask yourself these questions:

- What negative impact will sharing that information have on you?
- Does that person's success mean you will suddenly become a failure?
- If he/she gets that job or does that training, will you suddenly lose your job or not be paid your salary?
- If you recommend a drama class for your friend's daughter, will your daughter suddenly lose her talent?

- If you tell someone where you bought a beautiful dress or who your dressmaker is, will that dress no longer look nice on you?

I hope this sounds as ridiculous as it is intended to because that is exactly how it appears when we are competitive about things we should never be competitive about. It actually has the opposite effect, because it feels good to help others. That is how I feel whenever I do nice things for others.

An Asian or Jew will bring others into their business and show them the ropes. That is why you see many Asians in most organisations in the UK. There are often very few black people working in an organisation in the UK at a time. Maybe this is entirely coincidental, but I cannot help wondering if it is because the black people in that organisation refuse to recommend other black people for a job in that company.

I am able to draw that conclusion because several times I have told my black friends that there is a vacancy in my organisation and I want to refer a friend who is currently unemployed. This is the usual response I get.

Friend: Ah! That is risky o! What if he/she messes up and puts you in trouble? It is you they will blame.

Me: How can he/she mess up when they have so much experience in that profession?

Friend: Oh, that is even worse, they can even outshine you and take your job?

Me: but the vacancy is not even in my team or my department.

Friend: That does not mean he/she cannot turn against you. They will not appreciate it once they get in.

Me: How can they turn against me for helping them?

Friend: it is a competition nau! Anyway, I have told you. You cannot trust our people. Stop being too nice to them.

This is ridiculous isn't it? I did not allow it to deter me. I recommend people to my organisation and succeeded in getting some shortlisted for interviews. It is a win-win situation because you are helping someone and your organisation even rewards you with a recommendation fee if that person is hired. So, what is not to like? Other ethnic groups are making money from recommending their friends and helping them to boot. Black people are too worried about backstabbing to help a friend in need.

I have referred many friends and family to a very good training company for project management training. Someone asked me once if I was getting an incentive for the referral and they were surprised when I said no because I have never contacted the training company and they do not know who I am. I made the referral because some of my friends received good training at that company and were able to get great jobs afterwards. It should not be about the incentive.

There is a belief that black businesses like to monopolise the market location wherever they are. They do not want another black business in that vicinity offering the same product or service. Black businesses do not collaborate when they find themselves in close proximity to each other. This is the opposite for Jewish and Asian businesses.

Those ethnic groups collaborate and would even ask customers to visit the neighbouring Asian or Jewish shop if they do not have the item they seek. They go as far as calling the other shop on the phone to enquire if they have that item you seek. I have witnessed this a few times. A black business on the other hand would ask you to return a few days later for that item, so they could source it for you. They do not point you to their competitor.

As I have stated repeatedly in this book, it is foolish to generalise because not all black businesses behave the same way. Therefore, not all of them are competitive. I have a good story to share to buttress this point.

MY STORY

I shared a table with two other black authors at a business showcase event. One of them was a friend and well-known to me, while the other was unknown to me and I met her for the first time that day. We helped each other by selling each other's books when anyone visited our stall, especially when one of us was temporarily away from the stall. To us, we were a team, collaborating to sell our products. We did not focus on selling only our respective books, and we recommended each other's books. This was not planned or discussed beforehand, it just happened organically, and it was wonderful to see. We all sold many books that day. There was no jealousy or envy. It was such a great experience that we all came back the next year to do it again.

This collaboration meant a lot to me because I had an experience in the past when I shared a table with two white writers. Whenever anyone stood in front of our table to look at my books and ask questions about them, one of my fellow writers shouted that we were blocking the visibility of his books and asked us to move aside. We were sharing the same table, so where else should the customers stand? Whenever I sold a book, I would get even more hostility. That was an awful experience and I vowed never to share a table with other writers until I met those two lovely ladies.

HOW TO GET IT RIGHT

1. I hope the questions in this chapter have succeeded in making you see how silly it is to be competitive and unwilling to help others. Please let's lift each other up. We need our community to be more successful and we cannot do it alone.

2. I do agree that there are some bad people who turn against you after you bring them into your organisation, and I have heard stories like that. I chose not to be deterred by that because not everyone is bad. There are good and bad people in the world.
3. There are good people out there who deserve our help. Let's borrow a leaf from the non-black communities because they have some bad and untrustworthy people in their communities too, but they continue to collaborate and lift each other up as much as they can. We should do the same instead of competing and turning our backs on each other.
4. Our black community should not use the lack of collaboration as an excuse not to do business with a black business owner.

Chapter Twelve

The Myth That Black People Cannot Do Business

I think this is an unfair statement to make because of the many successful black businesses out there that are doing the right thing. So how did this school of thought come about? The evidence is attributed to the many terrible experiences of customers who patronise black businesses, coupled with the extensive list of the issues with business in the black community that we have discussed so far in this book. Aside from that, there were a few points raised by my respondents that I will highlight below.

SOME FACTORS THAT GIVE CREDENCE TO THIS MYTH

- Black businesses cannot do business because they do not draw up a contract. Whoever invented the word "GENTLEMAN'S AGREEMENT" or "WE SHOOK ON IT "must be a black man. We are too informal in the way we conduct business. Everything is usually done by word of mouth. Why not draw up a contract and get the agreement of the work to be delivered signed and agreed by both parties?
- We initiate partnerships without a partnership agreement. Even if that partnership is with a family member, there should always be a contract to protect each other in case of a conflict or dispute.
- We lend money to each other without paperwork. Therefore, we have nothing binding to hold on to when there is no repayment.

- We pay a lot of money for a service we do not understand and there is no contract to provide the necessary clarity on the work to be delivered.
- Even when contracts are signed, they are not honoured by the business owner. When the customer tries to enforce the contract, the business will do everything to break the contract.

KELVIN'S STORY

Kelvin always practised BLACK FIRST. He always finds a black-owned business to work with as long as the person is competent. He does not compromise on competence just because he wants to patronise a black business. If he does not find a black business to do that work, then he gives it to a non-black business. Kelvin is not put off by all the negative reviews and complaints about black businesses. I asked him how he is able to consistently do business with black businesses and he gave me one example and it made perfect sense.

He drew up a contract with an electrician to do a piece of work. The electrician was surprised and asked why he needed to sign a contract and Kelvin told him it was to protect both of them. Then, he agreed and they both signed it.

The contract contained a clause that upon completion of the work and the presentation of his electrician certificate, payment would be made. After completion of the work, the electrician asked for payment without presenting his certificate. The electrician said his certificate had expired and he forgot to renew it. Kelvin insisted on honouring the terms of the contract.

The electrician went to Kelvin's wife and Kelvin's mum to ask them to beg on his behalf so he could receive payment. He could not understand why a fellow black man like himself could be so strict about a contract.

Kelvin's wife did not bother to intervene because she understood her husband's stance and the fact that he was doing the right thing. His mum appealed to him and Kelvin refused to budge simply because he knew he would not be helping that electrician to do the right thing.

Then the electrician went to his brothers and asked them to beg Kelvin and when that did not work, the electrician went to the family pastor and he attempted to intervene. That did not deter Kelvin. In the end, the electrician was left with no choice but to go and renew his certificate as stipulated in the contract.

Kelvin believes we have a choice to demand that black businesses operate their businesses professionally as a condition for patronising their business and I could not agree more.

FRAMICHI PUBLICATIONS EXAMPLE

This is a black business that refuses to do any business with a client without a signed contract. Their services are book-writing coaching, ghostwriting and independent publishing. One word that sticks out in all their clients' testimonials is PROFESSIONAL. They do things properly from the start of a book project to its completion. Check out one of such testimonials and details of the company in the last chapter of this book.

IT IS NOT ALL BAD

Aside from the many amazing black businesses out there that are doing the right thing, there are some in the black community who are really good at running a business as we established in the previous section of this chapter. There is a belief that some in the black community like the Igbos from Eastern Nigeria have innate knowledge of business management and always do well in business. I disagree with that because it is not innate. No one is born to be a good entrepreneur.

The Igbos were nurtured to do that because those values were instilled in them at a young age. It is the environment in which they grew up too because the Igbos are known for their entrepreneurial spirit and skills. Running a business comes naturally to them because it is a dream many of them aim to actualise.

THERE IS ROOM FOR IMPROVEMENT

For other black tribes, it is a different ball game. It is difficult because that is not how they were nurtured. Running a business does not come easily to them. When you combine this difficulty with our value system that normalises bad behaviour and unethical practices, it is a recipe for disaster and failure.

Due to the fact that the majority of black businesses are not run properly, banks are reluctant to grant us business loans. They see our community as high risk and would rather lend to an Asian or non-black business than lend to a black business. We shall explore the issue of obtaining business finance in part three of this book.

HOW TO GET IT RIGHT

1. A contract is a way of doing things properly. Even if the black business owner does not draw up a contract, you the customer should request one.
2. Also, do not intervene when a business owner fails to honour a business contract and ask you to beg on their behalf. If we keep doing that nothing would change.

Chapter Thirteen

A Lack Of Education And Business Acumen Is To Blame

> ***"Business acumen**, also known as **business savviness**, **business sense** and **business understanding**, is keenness and quickness in understanding and dealing with a business situation (risks and opportunities) in a manner that is likely to lead to a good outcome."*
> *(Source: www.en.wikipedia.org)*

There is an argument that most black business owners lack the business acumen and education to run a successful business. Considering the fact that our value system places a high priority on university education, we know many of our black entrepreneurs are university graduates. Therefore, if the university education was the only factor or necessary factor, then those educated entrepreneurs should all be running successful businesses, right?

Well, there is some finesse and professionalism that comes from attaining a university degree and that is undeniable. It can in no way be compared to the way an uneducated person would run a business. That is apparent when dealing with some tradespeople and artisans. It appears some of them simply learnt a skill and decided to start trading by providing that service. (Hairdressers, tailors, barbers, builders, and carpenters come to mind). They are not educated in the art of entrepreneurship or how to run a business.

A survey carried out by the World Bank Enterprise in eight different African countries shows that university-educated entrepreneurs proved more successful at running a business.

"Do some black-owned firms grow faster than others? Owners' attainment of a university education was very important in determining the size of the firm (figure 3-4). We also observe that indigenous entrepreneurs with a university education started much larger firms than those that did not have a university degree in almost all of the countries surveyed. 1. University education appears to be correlated with a larger size at start-ups and a higher rate of growth for black-owned businesses. 2. There are three possible interpretations of the finding regarding the impact of university education: a university education provides an owner with the tools to run a firm; completion of a university degree reflects greater ability on the part of an owner and consequently greater potential for success of a firm; and a university degree enables an owner to access a network of other professionals who provide information or facilitates access to credit".

58 *Black Ownership of Businesses in Africa*

Figure 3-4. Average Current Firm Size, by Education of the Owner

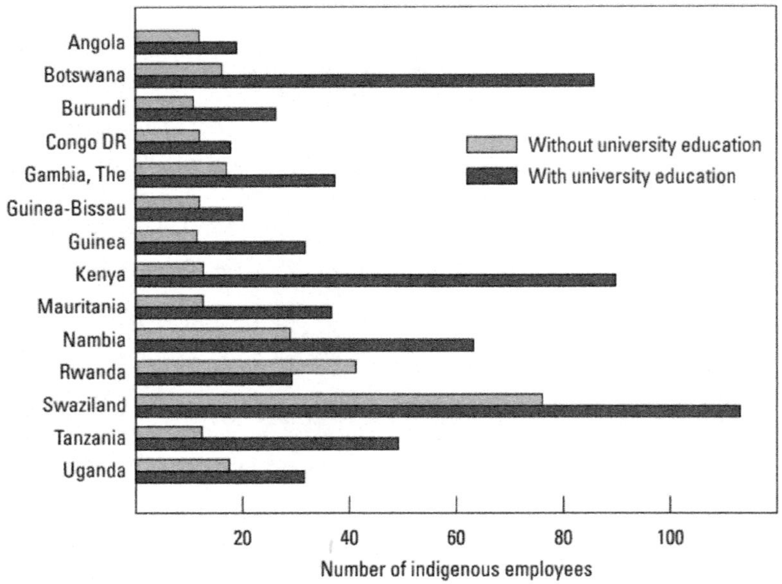

Source: World Bank Enterprise Surveys (www.enterprisesurveys.org).

(Source - www.cgdev.org)

It is clear that education is an incredible advantage to have as an entrepreneur. It can only make you better as an entrepreneur and good for your business.

That being said, there are educated business owners who are not business savvy. We have many tradesmen and artisans in our community who do not hold a university degree but are more business savvy than those who do.

Once again, the Igbo tribe in Nigeria comes to mind. They are nurtured to be entrepreneurs and coached by seasoned entrepreneurs. Many start out as apprentices and become very successful entrepreneurs. Therefore, I can conclude that being business savvy is also important and it is still the reason Igbo people make great entrepreneurs. Without education, a business-savvy person may lack the finesse and professionalism that is required to provide top-quality services and products. If you are educated and business savvy, then you have the full package. The sky is your limit.

HOW TO GET IT RIGHT

1. If you have a university degree (especially in a non-business discipline) and lack business acumen, then take some business courses to improve your skills.
2. If you have business acumen but are uneducated, then take some classes too to fill your skill gap. Go for training to learn the required soft skills of how to manage your business, especially customer service and professionalism, which are the two key things lacking in our black business community.

Chapter Fourteen

We Are Overly Critical Of Our Black Businesses

Are we excessively critical of black businesses?

This is an easy one. After reading all the preceding chapters buttressed with true life experiences about the feedback and experiences from black customers, can anyone honestly say we are overly critical of black businesses?

You only have to patronise five black businesses and see how many of them do exactly what the respondents say. I bet it would be all of them or four out of five at least. Unfortunately, it is that bad. Carry out this test.

Another respondent agreed that we know our problems as black people, so we do not need to write about them or share them with the world. I disagree with that because if we do not address our problems or highlight them how will there ever be a solution?

For most of the black entrepreneurs I interviewed it was not the negative feedback that bothered them, rather, it was the way the feedback was delivered. I agree with this entirely. If feedback is given nicely, constructively, and respectfully, it will be welcomed and accepted by the recipient. Do it in a positive manner. For example:

"If you do - - -, it will do - - - for your business "

CRITICISM FROM HATERS

There are definitely 'haters' and they are known for being hostile and aggressive with their feedback when that business does not deserve it. It could be out of envy and jealousy. If feedback is given this way, then it may not be accepted because it will come across as insincere. The black entrepreneur reacts by becoming defensive.

FEEDBACK IS A GIFT

I do agree that negative feedback is a difficult conversation to have, and it was not easy to write this book, but it has become imperative that we have these conversations. How else are we going to be competitive in the global marketplace? If we want to serve a diverse mix of customers from all ethnic groups, then we must improve our business standards. Our customers are not only black people; we should aim to do business with the whole world.

DO WE EXPECT TOO MUCH FROM BLACK BUSINESSES?

This is perhaps the most shocking thing to say because every customer expects good products and services from any business considering they have been paid for.

Does this mean black customers do not deserve the best service from black businesses? It should not come as a surprise that this school of thought is held by some black business owners that I interviewed. The good thing is that I only heard this from a very tiny number of respondents. That means it is not a widely held view.

Another respondent said black customers have to lower their standards when dealing with black businesses. Wow! Are our standards too high? Of course not, according to the majority of my respondents. If we can get better quality products and services from businesses of other ethnic groups, then we can demand the exact same quality of service from our people.

HOW TO GET IT RIGHT

1. My advice would be - do not be offended by the way the feedback was delivered. Instead, be receptive to it and review all the feedback to see if it is actually something your business is doing wrong. Do not be quick to disregard it. Think about it. You may learn one or two things. Tick off the ones that do not apply to you and fix the ones you can fix because it will improve your business.
2. Business owners should stop sweeping our problems under the proverbial 'carpet'. Have an open mind and consider the betterment of our community, and how we can improve the way we conduct business in our community. After all, the customer is always right, and we should do everything to make them think BLACK FIRST.

PART THREE

Black Businesses share their challenges

(Source - www.pxfuel.com)

Chapter Fifteen

Distrusted, Devalued And Negative Preconceptions

This is arguably the biggest challenge black business owners complained about. Negative preconceptions that black customers have about black businesses make running a business in the black community difficult. The Cambridge dictionary defines the word PRECONCEPTION as follows:

> *"an idea or opinion formed before enough information is available to form it correctly:"*
> *(Source - www.dictionary.cambridge.org)*

This means black customers have formed incorrect opinions about black businesses before doing business with them. All the black business owners I interviewed put this down as the biggest challenge they have to deal with. They complained of having to go out of their way to prove they can actually provide that service or product. Their word is not good enough.

There is an instant distrust that black business owners aren't who they say they are. They are either perceived as con artists who are going to scam customers or people who do not know what they are doing. The expectation is often that whatever service or product the customer pays for will not be delivered or substandard.

Anyone who grew up in Nigeria would know how consumers hate goods with the label "Made in Nigeria", and would try to avoid buying them if they can help it. This is because they believe the product to be substandard. The consumers prefer the more expensive imported goods that were not made in Nigeria.

Yes, we know where or how this preconception came about because we have addressed it in part one of this book. Nonetheless, black customers should give black businesses a chance and not be biased against them until they're given valid reasons.

As a black business owner, myself, I find this incredibly frustrating. Ponder my experience below:

MY STORY

As an author of five published books, a ghostwriter, book-writing coach and an independent publisher, I was organising a masterclass last year on how to write a book and get it published. My business consultant suggested that I should make a video to promote the event on social media and that I must hold five of my books to prove to the black people out there that I actually wrote five books.

Wo! I was reluctant to do this because I did not understand why anyone would expect me to lie about writing five books when my books are out there on Amazon and other global online bookstores for all to see. Therefore, I refused to do the video. A week later, I was holding a book signing session and

I noticed that most of the black people who approached my table asked me these questions:

- "Did you really write these books?"
- "Are you sure?"
- "Are you the author".
- "Really?"
- "Did someone ghostwrite it for you?"

Shocking! Imagine being asked such ridiculous and unnecessary questions. I had to repeatedly say 'yes, I wrote the book and that is my name on the cover'. I managed to convince some of them, and they ended up buying my books while some walked away with doubtful expressions on their faces. What was even more surprising is that when they move to the Caucasian authors beside me who I was sharing the table with those black customers did not ask them if they actually wrote their books.

How insulting and exasperating was that? It was disheartening to be the subject of such prejudice. It was at that point that I realised why my business consultant asked me to record that video to showcase my five books. I made the promo video reluctantly. The book writing and publishing masterclass was a success.

I am well known in my immediate community and network groups for what I do, but whenever I hold book signing events outside my town, black people still ask me those ridiculous questions, instead of asking me politely what the book is about like the non-black customers do. I have vowed never to do another promo video with my books in my hand just to prove a point to the black community that I am who I say I am.

EMEKA'S STORY

Emeka (not his real name) is a black business owner in England. He sells used cars he gets from auctions. He complained that black customers give him the runaround, asking him probing questions as though they are trying to catch him out in a lie because they have a preconceived notion that he would try to sell them a bad car. This is DISTRUST. They are also quite rude in the process.

Emeka stated a black customer has never bought a car from him. To his surprise, his white customers are serious buyers; they trust him, and are polite and professional towards him. Based on that he now prefers to deal with non-black customers.

MOBOLAJI'S STORY

This is an excellent example. Mobolaji (not his real name) is an accountant and owns a firm in England. As an honest black businessman, he treated his customers fairly and professionally. He was always sincere in his dealings with them. He told me what happened when he infomed a client that there was an overpayment and a refund had been made to the client's account. This was the response from the client:

> *"You gave me a refund? Really? Are you sure you are a Nigerian? I have never heard such a thing o! A Nigerian businessman giving me a refund. Thank you. Thank you very much".*

Mobolaji said he was stunned to hear that despite being aware of the issues with preconceptions and distrust. He asked his client why he assumed all Nigerian business owners were dishonest. The client apologised and said his assumption came from all the bad experiences he suffered in the past. Mobolaji advised him not to generalise because not all black businesses are dishonest. The client reluctantly agreed with him because of that refund.

This is one of the reasons why black businesses believe that even when they offer exceptional products and services to black customers, many refuse to give a testimonial, recommendation, or referral about it.

What more can I say here? Let's continue to do honest business with our clients so we can change that negative preconception and prejudice one business at a time.

UNWILLINGNESS TO PAY THE STANDARD PRICE

Many of the respondents complained that black customers never want to pay the standard price for anything. This is because they do not put much value on the service or product you provide and they always want to pay less and feel entitled to that lower price. Since the price you pay for something reflects the value you place on it, can this behaviour be interpreted to mean that black customers do not value black businesses and their products and services?

Or is it a cultural thing? I say this because in Africa, we haggle and negotiate the price of everything we buy in the market and that is our expectation. That being said, we do not haggle in superstores or supermarkets where an item has a listed price tag on it. That is why we do not haggle in supermarkets in the West, where everything has a listed price tag on it.

Does the absence of a price tag give us the right to haggle? I disagree with that because black customers do not haggle when they are dealing with non-black businesses. Most black customers think black businesses are overcharging them for that item and will haggle till the cows come home. The black businesses either end up giving in to that demand for a lower price or they walk away from the deal altogether.

In chapter six, we analysed how some black businesses have unjustifiably high prices for items, and many have priced themselves out of the market. That being said, you should consider what you're paying for and the value you are getting; pay the asking price so that the business can pay for the cost of delivering your order and also make a profit in the process.

FAMILIARITY BREEDS CONTEMPT

This problem of unwillingness to pay the standard price is much worse when black businesses deal with family and friends, because they expect an even bigger discount. In fact, friends or family usually expect to get that item for free or pay as little as possible.

It appears they do not value the effort and time put in to deliver that item just because they are your friend or family. Yet they will gladly pay the right fee if it was an unknown person or stranger, they were doing business with. That is why this section is aptly titled familiarity breeds contempt.

For this reason, many black businesses refuse to do business with a friend or family because it usually ends up destroying the friendship. If anything, a family or friend should pay even more to support that black businesses or leave a big tip.

Let's look at some true-life experiences.

PETER'S STORY

Peter asked a friend's son to be the DJ at his party. DJ Kay (not his real name) was a student. The fee was one hundred and twenty pounds and that was the standard fee. Peter thought because DJ Kay was a family friend and like a son to him, he should pay a lesser amount and he only paid DJ Kay one hundred pounds. DJ Kay accepted it reluctantly because Peter was like a father to him.

Sometime later Peter looked back at what he had done and he realised DJ Kay was like a son to him and he should have paid him even more than the standard fee. He knew he had taken DJ Kay for granted by paying him a lesser amount. If anything, he should be supporting that boy's business by paying him more. When DJ Kay graduated from university, Peter gave him a cheque for two hundred pounds and a gift too just to make up for it.

PAUL'S STORY

Kwame approached Paul, a black fund-raising consultant to help raise funds for his charity. It was time-consuming work that required a team and vast research, so Paul gave him a quote for nine thousand pounds. After much haggling and going back and forth on the price, Paul became fed up and decided not to continue with the negotiation because he could see that Kwame was not happy with the price.

Kwame went to a Caucasian fund-raising consultant and he was given a quote for thirteen thousand pounds. Surprisingly, Kwame paid that higher price. In the end, the Caucasian fund-raising consultant was unable to get the job done because he did not understand the black community.

Kwame came back to Paul to complain that the Caucasian fund-raising consultant did not raise any funds for him. He expected Paul to grab the opportunity to take on the work, but to his surprise, Paul turned it down and refused to work with him. Paul said he found it disrespectful that Kwame did not value his work enough to pay the lesser amount of nine thousand pounds but was happy to pay four thousand pounds extra to a Caucasian.

It was an inferiority complex that made Kwame believe the Caucasian could do a better job than a fellow black fundraiser. Kudos to Paul for walking away from this business deal and I think more black businesses should do the same. We should not accept such disrespectful treatment from any black client just to make some money.

HOW TO GET IT RIGHT

1. Walk away from any customer who does not value your products and services. Do not allow anyone to disrespect you.
2. You have to make a profit from your business because you incur expenses in the process. Anyone who cannot pay the right price can leave, as long as they are not being overcharged.

3. Do not avoid doing business with family and friends, but insist they pay the standard prices. Avoid any special treatment or discounts because of the relationship.
4. Trust black businesses until they give you a reason not to trust them. Black customers should have an open mind when they approach a black business. At least give a black business the chance to mess up before you write them off.
5. Customers should do their due diligence and be sure that the black business can provide the service before giving them the work. If you think the black business is incompetent, then look elsewhere. What you should not do is tarnish everyone with the same brush.
6. Remember there are bad businesses in every ethnic group. Scammers and fraudulent businesses are everywhere, but that has not stopped customers from trusting or valuing the businesses in their communities.
7. Do not generalise, because all black businesses are different. Remember they are managed by people from varied backgrounds and cultures. They have different values based on how they were raised and nurtured. I find that good, honest, and helpful people do business better than greedy and dishonest ones. Since I have met many people like this, please give them a chance and you will find many like Mobolaji around.

8. Black customers should stop the inferiority complex and mental slavery that makes them believe that non-black businesses are better and deserved to be paid more for the same products and services a black business can provide. Remember, cultural differences and understanding the black community are important factors in certain business services. Think carefully before making a decision about who to do business with.
9. As a black business, do not hesitate to ask for a testimonial from a customer who is happy with your service or product. I never stop asking my customers for testimonials and they give them to me because I work really hard to exceed their expectations. It is one way to know what they really think about your business.

Chapter Sixteen

Unethical Conduct

When it comes to unethical conduct during business dealings, it is not only the businesses that are the guilty parties. The black customers are also unethical in their actions. This is what black businesses have to say about it.

DISGRACEFUL BEHAVIOUR

Black customers receive goods and services but refuse to pay for it. It has resulted in many awkward arguments and shouting matches at business premises with the business owner insisting that payment must be made for the goods and services provided.

EDWIN'S STORY

A black customer ate at a restaurant and after eating everything on the plate, she pulled out a strand of hair from her wig and placed it on the plate. She claimed the hair was found in the food and refused to pay for it. This resulted in an argument and shouting match between the customer and the restaurant owner. Luckily, another customer sitting nearby noticed when this terrible customer put the strand of hair on the plate and challenged her about it to the restaurant's relief.

HOW TO GET IT RIGHT

Black Customers should not go into any business premises to shout and cause a scene. Whether you are right or wrong, your approach will determine the outcome of your request. Be polite and address the business staff with respect and they are likely to listen to you.

SEXUAL ADVANCES FROM CUSTOMERS

Some of the respondents complained about black customers flirting with them inappropriately, regardless of whether they were married or single.

They flirt with a business owner at the start of a business transaction just to get a discount or get that item for free. This is not always because they fancy the business owner or want to date him/her.

My research revealed that black female customers are more guilty of this than their male counterparts, and I understand some of these female customers do not stop at harmless flirting, but they go all the way. Check out Kofi's experience below:

KOFI'S STORY

Kofi owns a removals business in England. He told me how a few of his black and white female customers boldly offered him sex in exchange for his services. That's right! They offered him payment in kind. He was shocked at their behaviour and could not believe that any woman would do that, even married women.

I asked Kofi if this happened to him because he was a good-looking man and he said that was not the reason; these women did it to his friends in the same line of business. They just did it to avoid paying for the services. Kofi said it usually happens when the service is provided in the home of the customer. As a fellow black woman, I found this behaviour appalling to say the least. It is scandalous! Ladies, please do not do this. Kofi explained that this happens when the business owner is friendly with the female customers or flirts with them. Maybe that is perceived as the 'green light' those women need to proceed. I cannot help but blame the business owners for flirting with their female customers too; I guess both parties are guilty.

My question to business owners in this situation is this - DO YOU WANT TO GET PAID FOR YOUR SERVICES, OR GET LAID?

This brings me back to the issue of our value system as black people. These women could offer sex as payment to a fellow black person because they share the same value system. I doubt they would do the same thing with a non-black business owner.

SHOPLIFTING

Shoplifting is a universal problem. It is not limited to any ethnic group because it is an individual problem, irrespective of race. All over the world, business owners of retail stores have a process for dealing with shoplifting. Big stores have security guards at the EXIT to check for items bought without payment since the security tags on them would set off an alarm when the customer tries to leave the store. Stores also install CCTV cameras all over the store to record shoplifters in the act. In Costco, all receipts are checked by the security guards at the gate before customers leave the store to curb shoplifting. It is a big problem that is getting out of hand worldwide.

The police do not take it seriously because it is seen as a minor crime, and this has made shoplifters more aggressive and brazen in this criminal activity. For smaller businesses, it is even more difficult to keep under control.

JAMAICA

My research revealed that in Jamaica, black businesses suffer at the hands of shoplifters too, and some have taken even more drastic measures to curb it. In superstores in Jamaica, customers are required to leave their bags at the door upon entrance to prevent them from shoplifting and hiding items in their bags.

As though that wasn't bad enough, the refrigerators are remote-controlled, so the only way you can pick something from the fridge is if the staff opens the fridge to allow you pick the item you want.

IN PARTS OF AFRICA

In many parts of Africa, the most common way businesses tackle shoplifting is the installation of CCTV cameras and security features on most items on display. There is strategic display of light weight items where they are most visible. Since the heavier items cannot be lifted easily by shoplifters, they are displayed further inside the store.

Private security guards are hired to keep an eye on everyone going in and out of the store. The staff are also encouraged (compelled to act as security personnel too where necessary).

In Nigeria, jungle justice is meted out on anyone caught. It is instant lynching or severe beating before the police come in. Shoplifting is a serious offence there, and offenders have been known to be given a maximum of two years in prison, depending on the gravity of the offence. Lastly, this is a matter that depends on the ownership of such shops, and how far they intend to safeguard their businesses. Yet, it must be noted that only twenty percent of such crimes get to the police station, and that is if the police station is near the scene of the crime.

In addition, the complainant (the business owner) has to bribe the same police to do the job.

HOW TO GET IT RIGHT

1. If a customer fancies the business owner, the right thing to do would be to wait until after the business is concluded before making your feelings known. Otherwise, it is called taking advantage of the situation and exploiting it to your benefit.

2. This works both ways. Business owners should not flirt with a customer until after the business transaction is completed. Keep it professional and do not encourage such unethical behaviour.
3. I do not condone jungle justice. Lynching and beating up shoplifters is not the best way because it could result in a loss of life.
4. As a business owner, you have to explore a better and more professional way to deal with shoplifting in your store.

Chapter Seventeen

Challenges Obtaining Business Finance

"The vast majority of black-owned firms are very small businesses with fewer than ten employees. Many of these firms can be described as informal, operating on the margins of the private sector with very little working capital or other resources".
(Source - www.cgdev.org)

Obtaining business finance is perhaps the most important thing required to start a business or grow a business. Without start-up capital, a business will never get off the ground. Without business finance, an entrepreneur cannot lease office premises, hire staff, or buy equipment and supplies. Money is required every step of the way. Depending on the type of business, the start-up capital may be quite high. So how do you raise the funds to start a business?

From the preceding chapters, we have come to understand how most black businesses struggle to cope with financial constraints. They put up prices just to make enough money to meet their costs. They cannot afford to hire staff because they do not have the funds to pay for it.

We have also learned that our community do not know how to collaborate in business as the Asians do. They prefer to go at it alone, which means carrying one hundred percent of the risk. The result is inadequate funds, and this ends up in a short-lived business.

So how can black businesses obtain finance? This is usually in the form of a business loan or business credit card. The only place to get these are banks or other financial institutions.

Black businesses find it difficult to obtain finance from banks due to prejudice. For a long time, banks refused to give business loans to black businesses. A small business loan in the UK ranges from one thousand pounds to twenty-five thousand pounds.

The black business respondents informed me that wherever they are in the world i.e. Africa, UK, USA and the Caribbean, banks were known to be unwilling to lend to black businesses and even when they do, the interest rates are usually higher than the standard rates. So, is there really prejudice? Let's dig further.

UNITED KINGDOM

I had the privilege of interviewing an old member of the Yorkshire Black Enterprise Convention who informed me that the Yorkshire Black Enterprise Convention carried out a study from 2004 - 2005 into why there was such a low number of black businesses start-ups and why the few existing businesses could not thrive.

The outcome was a lack of business finance which they allegedly could not get from the banks at the time. The convention presented its findings to the Yorkshire Enterprise Commission, and this led to an improvement in the situation; few of the banks started to lend to black businesses from the African and Caribbean communities. However, it appeared only two of the high street banks were actively lending to the black community (I can attest to this because I was working as a Business Specialist at one of those two high street banks during that period and I packaged business loans for customers from all ethnic backgrounds and there was no discrimination. If there was I did not notice). The study confirmed that the other high street banks were alleged to only lend to Asians in the BAME (Black, Asian, and Minority Ethnic).

It did not stop there. Under Prime Minister Tony Blair, the Labour government took active steps to support the BAME communities by introducing the ENTERPRISE SCHEME. This made it easier for more black businesses to get business loans, but the banks had the last say on this; they could decide who to lend to, and how much interest to charge for the credit facility.

THE HIGH LENDING COST

When banks started to lend money to black businesses, it was a great relief. However, the interest rates were discovered to be higher than those charged for loans to non-black businesses. This was once again proven by the research conducted by the Yorkshire Black Business Enterprise Convention.

They discovered that out of every ten black businesses that received small business loans from banks, nine of them were charged a seven and a half per cent interest rate and only one had a lower interest rate of five per cent. How were these businesses expected to pay back loans with such high-interest rates? By raising their prices, and selling everything they could in their stores. We have read a few examples of this already in this book.

This is residual racism and prejudice against black businesses. So, what was the reason for that? Allegedly, the banks discovered that out of every five black businesses who took business loans, only two used the funds for the right purposes. Some of the respondents gave examples of male friends who took a loan and travelled abroad for six months to do something else. Another business owner bought a flashy Mercedes Benz car with the money. So why did they take the loan or even start the business in the first place? Many did the right thing by using the funds to improve their business.

I do agree that this is wrong, but these black businesses are not the only ethnic group guilty of this. Some in the non-black ethnic groups do the same. Sadly, it became the reason for the prejudice against black businesses. Why punish a whole community for the sins of a few? I learned that banks consider us high-risk, and this is still a view held by UK banks today.

I must point out that I cannot confirm or deny this issue of higher interest rates charged to black businesses. When I worked in the banking industry in the UK it was not flagged up and none of the bank's black business customers made a complaint about it.

USA

The black community in the United States of America suffer a worse fate than their British or African counterparts. I interviewed some black business owners, and they confirmed that in America, prejudice against black businesses is endemic. The black community has had to deal with more than just prejudice from the banks. They have lost their lives and destruction of businesses. The following is a well-known example:

> *"The **Tulsa race massacre**, also known as the **Tulsa race riot** or the **Black Wall Street massacre**,[12] was a two-day-long massacre that took place between May 31 and June 1, 1921, when mobs of white residents, some of whom had been appointed as deputies and armed by city government officials,[16] attacked black residents and destroyed homes and businesses of the Greenwood District in Tulsa, Oklahoma. The event is considered one of the worst incidents of racial violence in American history.[17][18] The attackers*

burned and destroyed more than 35 square blocks of the neighbourhood–at the time one of the wealthiest black communities in the United States, colloquially known as "Black Wall Street".

(Source - www.en.wikipedia.com)

The Black Wall Street was the racially motivated destruction of the 'wealthiest black communities' in the USA, which could be interpreted to mean that the white supremacists did not want black people to do well in business. Unsurprisingly, black businesses struggle to get finance from banks to help with their business. It was not until Barack Obama introduced the small business Loan Administration that things began to improve.

"Since the beginning of 2009, through the Recovery Act and the Small Business Jobs Act, the Small Business Administration (SBA) has approved 334,815 loans, supporting close to $163 billion in lending for small businesses. The SBA under President Obama has helped push more capital out the door than any other administration over a comparable time period."

(Source - www.obamawhitehouse.archives.gov)

That says it all. The SBA also offered training and support to small businesses in the USA, not just black businesses.

Thanks to Obama, many black men and women are running successful businesses today. Black female business owners are more successful than their male counterparts because they are manufacturers of beauty products for skin care and hair care. Black American male business owners are less successful because they are mainly service providers, and they have to compete with more established companies.

I must point out that African Americans like to have a good time too, and some take the loan and go on a shopping spree to enjoy themselves. Maybe it is a male thing amongst our black men because black women seem more focused and spend money wisely on their businesses, and this may be another reason why they are more successful entrepreneurs in America than their male counterparts.

AFRICA

A survey conducted across eight countries in Africa by the World Bank Enterprise revealed that banks and financial institutions in Africa, the ancestral home of the black race, are less likely to give a loan to indigenous companies compared to their foreign non-black business counterparts, but it is due to creditworthiness and other considerations.

"Do indigenous firms have less access to credit? That is the key question. Are they less likely to have bank accounts, overdraft protection, and loans? Is access to the banking sector correlated with financial depth? Or are banks simply sorting firms according to their creditworthiness? In almost all the countries in our sample, we see that indigenous firms have less access to overdraft protection than minority-owned firms (figure 3-5).3 But the data also present evidence suggesting that the financial sector sorts firms to determine their creditworthiness"

Black Ownership of Businesses in Africa **59**

Figure 3-5. Firms with Overdraft Protection, by Ethnicity

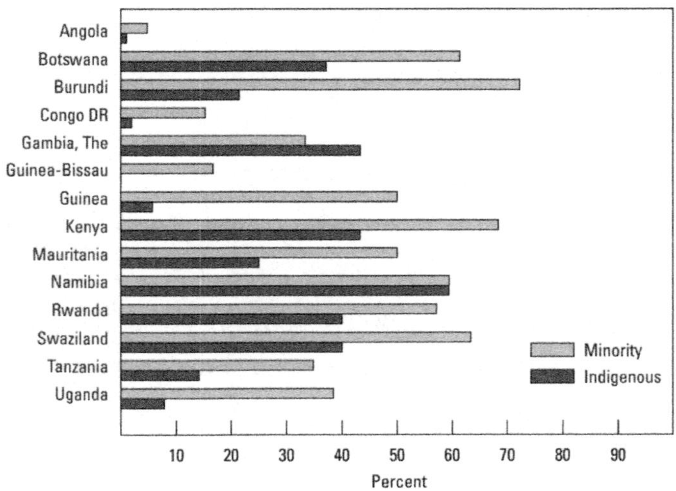

Source: World Bank Enterprise Surveys (www.enterprisesurveys.org).

Figure 3-6 shows that there also are big differences in the percent of firms with audited accounts when disaggregated by ethnicity. Similarly, indigenous firms are less likely than minority-owned firms to own their business premises; consequently, they have less collateral with which to obtain financing (figure 3-7). These firms are less likely to be creditworthy and so have less access to finance".

60 *Black Ownership of Businesses in Africa*

Figure 3-6. Firms with Audited Accounts, by Ethnicity

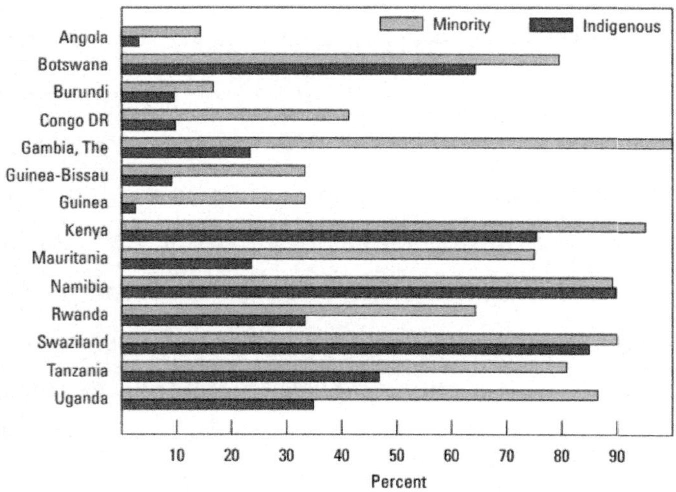

Source: World Bank Enterprise Surveys (www.enterprisesurveys.org).

www.cgdev.org

HOW TO GET IT RIGHT

1. It is right to conclude that 'one bad apple has spoilt the whole bunch'. We have seen how our attitude to business lending has further fuelled the prejudice against our business community by the banks and financial institutions.

2. It is simple. Let's pause and consider the consequences of our actions, and how misusing a business loan or not paying it back can become a major barrier to a fellow black business who really needs the funds and has good intentions of spending it on their businesses.

3. Most importantly, black entrepreneurs should meet all the bank's criteria for business finance. You have to do things by the book. Register your business and receive payments into your business account. For a startup you need a business plan. If you are an existing business, you may require Audited Accounts to get some types of business finance. The key point here is to ensure you go to the bank prepared. Do not give them the chance to decline your loan application.

4. Lastly, entrepreneurs should adhere to the legislative requirements relevant to their business sector to ensure they are eligible for other available support from the government.

Chapter Eighteen

Employees Wrecking The Business

I devoted a chapter to this problem of untrained employees we find at most business premises. Some businesses do not have employees at all. You find many black small business owners struggling to do everything alone and the business suffers as a consequence of that. In chapter seven the absence of an employee contributed to the collapse of Stella's business in less than twelve months.

I interviewed many black business owners about this issue and they all said the same thing - they do not trust their black employees and it is for the following reasons:

- Stealing
- Lying
- Showing up late to work or not showing up at all
- Bring their personal problems to work
- Unprofessional attitude despite training
- High staff turnover
- Laziness

When I heard these reasons, my first question was this: "Did you hire the right person for the job? Were they vetted? Did you obtain references?" The answer I received from the black business owners in Africa was that it is easier to do reference checks in the West than it is in Africa because recruitment practices have better systems in place to enable this.

UNETHICAL CONDUCT OF EMPLOYEES

In Africa, even when you obtain references and a guarantor, most employees still steal and try to wreck the business. The business owners could not understand why someone who was desperate for a job and pleaded to be hired, would steal from their employer. The employees who steal and lie are kicked out of the job, only to be replaced by new employees who do the same thing.

I asked if the employees were paid the right wages. Although that is not an excuse or a justification for stealing, I just wanted to understand the reason for the theft.

The business owners said it does not matter how much you pay them; they steal all the same. This is prevalent with retailers of groceries and food items. From restaurants to bakeries and clothing stores, the stealing is the same.

BODE'S STORY

Bode owns a bar and restaurant in Lagos, NIGERIA. The first problem he noticed in his staff was their lazy attitude towards their work. They would sit in the back rooms, playing on their phones instead of attending to customers. Bode spent time training them in the art of customer service and customer satisfaction. His staff only did the right thing when he was on the premises. As soon as he left the premises, they returned to lazing around.

The other problems Bode had with his staff were lying and stealing. He'd noticed food ingredients he had bought in bulk often ran out quicker than expected. He asked the chef and kitchen staff, and no one gave a good explanation for the reason why the items ran out so quickly.

Bode secretly installed CCTV cameras around the restaurant and was surprised to see some of his employees stealing food items. When he informed the guilty staff that they were caught stealing, they denied it until he showed them the video evidence. He fired them and replaced them with a new team, but the stealing continued.

Bode's recruitment process involved placing an advertisement in front of his restaurant that he was hiring. Anyone who walked in to apply for the job was interviewed and if successful, they were offered the job on the spot. It was a simple but risky process because no strict vetting procedures were applied.

When Bode returned to the UK to spend time with his family, he constantly monitored his staff via the CCTV to see if they were doing the right thing. He was always on edge and agitated, all because he had employees he could not trust. Since he started the business his wife constantly worried about his blood pressure.

Bode never called the police to arrest any of his employees. He reprimanded them and when they did not change, he replaced them.

I am still at a loss as to why employees steal, because they end up losing that job and the income that comes with it. So why steal at all when it never ends well? It is self-sabotage.

I have to blame this once again on our value system. In Africa, stealing and corruption have been normalised because we have corrupt politicians embezzling government funds and resources with no consequences. Instead, they are celebrated like heroes and admired by sycophants for their wealth. Since there are no consequences to act as a deterrent, stealing has become the norm in many black communities in Africa.

I worked in the banking sector in Nigeria for a few years after graduating from university and I can confirm that reference checks and due diligence were done for all the jobs I did in Nigeria. Since I worked in large corporations (mainly banks), this leads me to conclude that small and medium-sized businesses in Africa may be the ones most affected by the issues highlighted here. It makes sense because if you have the funds, you can hire the best people for your business wherever you are in the world.

CHEAP LABOUR

Black businesses in the West have no excuse for not employing the right workers because there are advanced technology and systems in place for recruitment. So why don't they take advantage of it? Those I interviewed complained that they too could not find the right people. I asked them the same question about paying the right salary, or employing someone from an agency.

The answer from some UK black entrepreneurs was that they could not afford to meet all the requirements of a National Insurance contribution and Pension contribution as well as the salary. So, they have resorted to hiring cheap labour on zero-hour contracts anywhere they can find them.

If this cheap labour is the reason for the poor service we receive at many of our black business premises, then we can conclude that "the businesses definitely pay for what they get". If you want good and honest employees, you have to go through a recruitment agency so they can perform due diligence and vet those people before you employ them.

I can empathise with these black businesses because the cost of running a business is very high, especially when you require a physical business premises and on-site staff.

CHALLENGES WITH TRAINING

How about training? Even If you hire cheap labour, you can train them to offer better service, right? The respondents said they offer training, but the calibre of people they hire is the problem. They do not adapt properly to the work environment, and to dealing with customers. If they are unhappy or troubled, they wear it on their faces, and everyone in the workplace knows about it, even the customers.

EMPLOYING FAMILY MEMBERS (NEPOTISM)

Many black businesses have employed family members to help run their business and the outcome has been proven to be much worse in many cases. Employed family members have a sense of entitlement; because it is a family business, they believe they can do exactly as they wish. They take the business owner for granted. Many have embezzled funds and run businesses to the ground.

A good friend of mine living in England set up a bakery and superstore in Nigeria and appointed his brother as the general manager of the business. He was so excited when he set up those two businesses. He told me last year that he had to shut down both businesses because his brother mismanaged them. There was so much stealing going on that the once highly profitable businesses were making consistent losses. He is still heartbroken about it. This caused a big rift in the family. He threatened to take his brother to court, but their parents and extended family intervened, and they always say these words.

> *"How can you sue your brother to court? He is family."*

There are so many cases in Africa of family members destroying a business that was set up by a sibling or parent who lives abroad. I have even seen a few sad videos about it on TikTok. I am yet to hear a good outcome of a family member running a business successfully in the absence of the owner. This continues to baffle me because your family should want your business to be successful, especially when that business is their source of income. They forget that once that business is gone, their income stops as well.

MY STORY

I have an experience of this which is closer to home. My uncle lived in Benin City, located in the midwestern part of Nigeria. He set up a beer distribution business in our hometown, which was only three hour's drive from Benin-city. He put his brother in charge of the business, to manage it on his behalf. My uncle said he did this to help his brother because he needed a source of income, and also because his brother lived in the town.

My uncle visited the town every weekend to check on the management of the business. Despite that, his brother wrecked the business all the same. He made sales and spent the money on himself instead of paying the suppliers to restock the items. My uncle had no choice but to shut down the business, his investment gone down the drain. My uncle was so angry that he punched his brother. There was a huge fight about it.

In the end, the whole family intervened, and he was asked to forgive his brother because they were family. I cannot help but wonder if my uncle's brother had the necessary skills to run that type of business. Were such reasons considered when my uncle handed over the business to his brother? This is one of the reasons why collaboration and business partnerships are so difficult to establish in the black community.

If the business owner is present and working side by side with the employee family member, then there may be a better outcome.

HOW TO GET IT RIGHT

1. I believe a lot of the problems black businesses have with their employees is the recruitment processes. Find a way to recruit the right people and be prepared to pay a better wage for it.
2. The cost to you of hiring cheap labour or dishonest family members is too high, as shown above. It could mean the end of your business.

The choice is clear - invest more in good, capable employees or lose your business and peace of mind.

Chapter Nineteen

Black Business Partnerships

"The keystone of successful business is cooperation. Friction retards progress."
- James Cash Penney

The issue of our inability to have successful business partnerships in our community originates from our inability to collaborate as black people. I have addressed this in part two of this book.

This time, I want to highlight what black business owners say about their challenges with forming partnerships. Many of the respondents put it down to an inherent lack of trust that stems from the time of the slave trade. Is this true? Ponder this:

WHY PARTNERSHIPS FAIL

Why was the partnership formed? Some respondents complained that they entered into a partnership to make quick money, and for others, it was for a long-term investment. Those in it for the quick profit said they wanted to take the profit out and spend it on themselves because they felt it was their reward for months of hard work, but their business partner wanted the profit to be invested back into the business and to wait for at least two years before enjoying the gains.

When one partner refused, it became a conflict, so the others would either connive to oust, undermine, or swindle them. It always came down to the money in the context of long-term vs short-term thinking. This is one of the reasons why black people do not do partnerships very well.

Many business partnerships collapse because one party leaves the business out of frustration. This is often because one party sees themselves as the boss or the leader and believes they should come first whenever it matters.

Everyone wants to be the boss in the partnership due to our big egos. Hello! It is a partnership, which means you both have equal rights and equal shares unless one holds more shares than the other. This is where a partnership agreement comes in; it should be understood, documented, and signed by all parties. The share structure should be defined early on too. Who owns the majority shares? Is it fifty-fifty? This structure is very important and not having this agreement in place could make or break your business partnership.

The fact that most black people see themselves as competitors is the bane of our community. Even when they own and manage a business together or have a well-defined partnership in place, it does not put a stop to our desire to compete against each other. Partners are meant to be a team, so what is the point of the competition?

Many respondents complained that they entered into partnerships with friends without considering if both parties were a good fit, shared the same vision and most importantly agreed on the WoW (ways of working). The friends in the partnership 'tiptoed' around each other. They avoided the difficult conversation of telling their business partner that they were performing below expectation or making wrong decisions even to the detriment of the business.

Why do they have a problem with honest feedback or opinion? Especially when that feedback or opinion could save the business from financial loss. This is made worse if the partners are introverts who would do anything to avoid a confrontation. A partnership made up of a mix of straight-talking people and those unwilling to have honest and open conversations will find it difficult to work together, and the outcome would be a dissolution of the partnership.

WHY DO NON-BLACK BUSINESSES DO PARTNERSHIPS BETTER THAN US?

How does the Indian community collaborate? An Indian man tells his parents that there is a flat down the road that he would like to buy for a buy-to-let business. His parents rally around their extended family to raise the funds as a loan for that young man. There is no jealousy or envy. The young man buys the house, renovates it into two to three flats and rents them out. Two years later, he releases the equity on that house to buy a second house and so it goes on until he becomes a property magnate owning several properties.

Of course, by now he has paid off the loan and is driving around in a flashy Mercedes Benz, to the envy of those who do not know how he made his money. The added bonus is that this young man is also able to create jobs for those in his community from that investment.

Asians and Jews draw up contracts and partnership agreements and they agree to be taken to court if they fail to honour the agreement. It doesn't matter if they are brothers or relatives.

Do that as a black person and our community will call you a bad person for taking your relative to court. The black family or friends know this, and they will fail to honour the business agreement and get away with it.

What happens if a black man goes to his extended family and community to ask for this kind of support? Or if he asks them to join forces with him to do a buy-to-let business. He does not get the money or financial support. The response is usually this:

"So na only you come England to make money? Or I come London to look London Bridge?"

This shows that there is too much envy and jealousy in our black community. One of the black relatives will take that business idea and try to copy it or do it for themselves even if they do not fully understand how it is done. Most times, they will struggle at it, and the young man who had the brilliant idea in the first place and would probably have been successful at it never achieves his dream. So, less business success in the family all round.

Looking at the above comparison, it is easy to guess which of these two communities are thriving and achieving immense business success. Asians, Arabs and Jews form business clusters very well and the closest we have to this is the Igbo tribe from Nigeria. They do so in Nigeria or where you have many of them trading. (We have covered the entrepreneurial spirit of the Igbos in previous chapters.)

THE ASIAN BUSINESS PARTNERSHIP STRATEGY

Asian business owners pull money together to start a business and work hard to make it a success. Then they open a few branches of that business and the other partner heads it. They trust each other and work well in partnerships.

The black community does not do this. We prefer to go at it alone, and sometimes the business fails because the Jewish or Asian competitor next door operates their business better and opens even more shops down the road and corners the entire market for that product or service. A good example is the African grocery stores and the Afro hair products retail stores.

THE STORY OF TWO BROTHERS

One of my respondents told a story of two brothers who were pastors. They set up two separate churches that were three miles apart. When they were asked why they did not join forces to set up one church, the eldest asked what the sharing formula for the tithes/donations would be. Was this not meant to be a church? Why is the focus on the money to be made? Everyone in the black community wants to be the boss, to be a business owner instead of collaborating and working together to make a success of a joint venture.

A DIFFERENT TYPE OF PARTNERSHIP

There are various forms of business partnerships. Check this out:

TRACEY'S STORY

I spoke to a black business owner who owns a fully functional hairdressing salon in London. Tracey (not her real name) is not a hairdresser herself, so she leases chairs and equipment in her salon to hairdressers and barbers who provide the services. Tracey signed a contract agreement with them to pay her a certain amount weekly.

For the first few weeks of the contract agreement, some of the hairdressers and barbers lied to Tracey that they were off sick and had not been at work the entire week. They said this so they would not have to pay her for the full week. Tracey believed her hairdressers and barbers and empathised with them. She did not suspect they were lying to her until a friend of hers mentioned that the hairdresser who complained of absence from work due to ill health was the same person who styled her hair on the purported sick day.

Tracey secretly installed a CCTV camera in her salon and observed that the hairdressers worked every day without a day off, not even on Sundays. That was when she knew the hairdressers had been lying to her to avoid paying her the right rental fee as agreed when they signed the contract.

Yes, it is not easy for black business owners to do business in our community. They are often faced with distrustful partners every step of the way.

HOW TO GET IT RIGHT

1. Be professional about everything and pretend you are working in an organisation for someone else and not your own company. Black People tend to behave better at their jobs than they do when they are running their own businesses. That is the only way to maintain an appropriate level of professionalism which is often missing in many black business owners.
2. Be careful when you chose business partners. Sharing the same vision or agreeing on the vision is not good enough because visions change along the way.

3. It is even more important to agree on the WoW, otherwise, there will be disagreements. Since disagreements are inevitable, a clear code of conduct and conflict resolution procedure must be put in place before that partnership commences.
4. Be careful when going into business with people you barely know or who are just acquaintances. It is hard enough with people you know, so imagine a partnership with strangers.
5. Even when doing business with your friends and family, do not take them for granted or be unprofessional with them.
6. It is not a friendship, it is a business, so treat it like one.
7. Beware of sexism and do not place the responsibility of carrying out operational tasks on the women in the partnership.

Chapter Twenty

The Conclusion – Unsung Heroes Of Black Business

If we treat our business with the same seriousness and professionalism we exhibit at our paid employment, that may be the solution.

I came to this conclusion because most black people tend to conduct themselves professionally or try really hard when they are in employment. That is what I consider the GOLDEN RULE FOR BLACK BUSINESSES

Why else do most black people go early to work when it is a paid job but go late to every event or business appointment when they are business owners? We collaborate and work well with others in teams at work, therefore we know it can be done. If we can do it in our places of employment, then we should be able to do it at our businesses too.

THE FUTURE

Maybe all the problems we have in our community is age specific. The older generation do things differently from the younger generation. Our generation conducts business differently from the way generation Z does it. Just like we are conducting business better than our fathers and ancestors did it. I believe black businesses are evolving and will continue to improve and I look forward to it. As a business owner myself, I am trying to run an exemplary business and every time I get those amazing testimonials from my clients for my professionalism, I know there are many like me out there trying to do the same thing.

This probably explains why we have many successful black entrepreneurs in the food and hospitality industry in the UK at the moment. There is a boom in black restaurants, Lounges, and nightclubs businesses. The quality of the products and services on offer are great and the entrepreneurs are working hard to give their customers the best. I have patronised many of them on a night out and thoroughly enjoyed myself. This leads me nicely to the last section of this book.

KUDOS TO SOME UNSUNG HEROES OF BLACK BUSINESS EXCELLENCE

It appears black customers are a bit reluctant to share their testimonials or recommendations with black businesses. There are fantastic black businesses out there doing amazing things, but they do not get testimonials and recommendations. That is why I have named them aptly as unsung heroes of black business excellence.

If a black business has served you brilliantly, exceeded your expectations or delighted you in the course of doing business with them, it is very important to tell them about it because we have to keep encouraging our black businesses to excel at what they do.

That is why I have devoted the last section of this book to showcase some awesome testimonials that respondents and friends shared with me about black businesses who CONSISTENTLY deliver excellent products and services.

O42 RESTAURANT AND BAR

"042 Restaurant in Leytonstone, London is great. I always go there to buy grilled fish (Crocker or/and Tilapia, depending on which me and the Mrs fancied). Their service on a cool evening weekdays, without the weekend club distraction, is second to none. Your order is taken and delivered fast and courteously with no extended waiting time. The grilled fish and plantain with fried yam as extra/side order is to die for. I could eat it every day 😊. The way it's prepared.....slow grilled in the oven and garnished with peppers and flavours is heavenly. The finished product is succulent and tickles the taste buds like no other. Need I go on? Cheers!"

- *Austin*

"The determination and drive to succeed by the owners of 042 is commendable. Consistency in the quality of food.' Opening of other related businesses e.g. restaurant, bed & breakfast, relaxation lounge etc"

- *Ed*

(Business website - www.042loungehtx.com)

VBO EXCLUSIVE LOUNGE

"The interior decor and facilities in the lounge is impressive including the conveniences. There is a strong focus and emphasis on clients having a good time"

- *Ed*

"This is currently the best and number one nightclub in the UK. A favourite of the black community. The music and ambiance are second to none. VBO is a trailblazer "

- *Franca*

(Business website - www.vbolounge.co.uk)

PATRICE BAILEY INTERNATIONAL

"My testimonial would be seeing the way Patrice Bailey communicated the essence and structure of her business endeavours is something worthy of emulation - processes, systems and procedures that supports what she does in business including clear and unambiguous communication to her diverse clients. Personally, I think this is something most African businesses struggle to contend with because of "cultural norms and practices" which they've even exported into western countries. Then you wonder why our customers are "we we"!"

- *Ritchie*

(Business website - www.patricebaileyintl.com)

NANAVAN LTD.

"Great customer service. Even in the rain, wet and slippery, my priced belongings were packed and carefully transported to my new home without any breakage/damage. A very professional service with competitive pricing. Thank you, very impressed."

- *Matilda*

"Nanavan Ltd is my go-to whenever I move home. They offer an all-inclusive package. Aside from the removals of your belongings, they go the extra mile to install your electrical gadgets and furniture at no extra cost. It is an exceptionally helpful service that I have not found with most removals companies".

- *Franca*

(Business website - not yet available)

LIMELIGHT SECURITY & SERVICES LTD

"They've set a very high standard of professionalism. All their staff are highly trained and experienced. We used them for a wedding as security, making sure only invited guests were allowed in the venue since an afrobeat star was performing at the reception. Carried out the job to a perfect T. Their staff were respectful and polite whilst also being assertive at the

same time. Those denied entry didn't feel offended. Would recommend them to anyone with security needs".

- *Austin*

(Business website - www.limelightsecurity.co.uk)

FRAMICHI PUBLICATIONS LTD

"A credit and thanks to Framichi Publications for the way it got my book published. Great professionalism was displayed from our first virtual session. I had a system glitch at my end, the first 45 minutes was spent fixing the connection problems. Franca encouraged me until we could see and hear each other. She clearly explained the process of book publishing, she gave the various options available, their pros and cons with no hard selling of her services. I was given time to assess the options before deciding to go with Framichi Publications. The rest is history as the book, Burning the Wealth of a Nation, The Nigeria Perspective was successfully published by Framichi Publications late in July 2023. I recommend Framichi Publications for their expertise, they will ensure that detailed attention is paid to all aspects of your book. Framichi will get you book published in good time."

- *Michael Famokunwa - Author of Burning the Wealth of a Nation, the Nigeria Perspective (2023)*

"Thank you to my book writing coach, Franca B. Lawrence, who has made my dream of writing this book become a reality. Thank you for encouraging me, supporting me and cheering me on when I was on the brink of slowing down and procrastinating. Your calm, pleasant professional approach to the way in which you conducted the coaching, assisted in bringing out the best in me. You created a wonderful writing experience that made me feel confident and able to achieve much more than I had ever imagined. Grateful to have shared my writing journey with you as my writing coach. Happy to recommend you every time."

- *Carmen Cameron - Author of SURVIVOR (2023)*

(Business website- www.Framichipublications.com)

I hope these examples of excellent black businesses have inspired you to improve your business practices. I do not have all the answers, but I have done my bit for our community. It is your turn now. This book is out there to help you figure it out for yourself, as a black business or black customer.

Good luck and I wish you success always in all your endeavours.

ABOUT THE AUTHOR

F B Lawrence is a six-time published author, ghostwriter, and book-writing coach. She is passionate about book writing and thinks it is the coolest thing in the world. F B Lawrence is the author of *The ZEANN Gang, Bully Busters'* series of children's fiction novels. Also check out her widely acclaimed book, *A Carriage Full of Laughs.*

F B Lawrence holds a master's degree in creative writing from Teesside University, United Kingdom. She is the CEO/ Founder of Framichi Publications, and she lives in England with her family.

For more information about the author and upcoming book releases, please visit her websites:

www.framichipublications.com

www.francablawrence.com